# SPORTS QUIZ TIME... DOWN MEMORY LANE...

Come on along, fans! You're older than you think. You can remember more things about sports than you thought. And if you don't actually remember, you'll have read or heard about those famous stars and events from yesteryear. This is the quiz book that has it all—the fabulous personalities, from Wilt Chamberlain and Johnny Unitas to Ted Williams and Muhammad Ali; some booed, most cheered; memorable competitions; fantastic facts; crazy events, funny names, coveted awards, zany characters, and all sorts of electrifying happenings at stadiums, fields, bowls, courts, alleys, and courses.

**THE SPORTS NOSTALGIA QUIZ** is itself a great *new* sport. And you don't need a superdome to play it—just a minute between innings, at the corner bar, at parties, or during rainouts.

You'll be able to stump your friends in no time!

# SIGNET Books You'll Enjoy

☐ **THE SPORTS NOSTALGIA QUIZ BOOK by Zander Hollander and David Schulz.** The wide world of sports—from yesteryear to yesterday—over 150 quizzes for fans of all ages!
(#Y6318—$1.25)

☐ **THE ILLUSTRATED SPORTS RECORD BOOK by Zander Hollander and David Schulz.** Here, in a single book, are 350 records with stories and photos so vivid they'll make you feel that "you are there." Once and for all you'll be able to settle your sports debates on who holds what records and how he, or she, did it. (#E6682—$1.75)

☐ **THE COMPLETE HANDBOOK OF PRO BASKETBALL, 1977 EDITION edited by Zander Hollander.** Here's your chance to get 22 Pro Team Yearbooks combined into 1 in the only guide and record book you'll need to follow the 1976-77 season—in the arenas or on TV! Included are 22 NBA Scouting Reports, Rosters, Player Profiles, Statistics, Schedules, TV/Radio, Photos, All-Time Records and lots more!
(#J7198—$1.95)

☐ **THE COMPLETE HANDBOOK OF PRO HOCKEY, 1977 EDITION edited by Zander Hollander.** Here's your chance to get 29 NHL and WHA Team Yearbooks in 1 in the only guide and record book you'll need to follow the 1976-77 season ... in the arenas or on TV! Included are NHL and WHA Scouting Reports—Profiles—Rosters—All-Time Records—Great Moments—TV/Radio, Photos, Career Records and lots more! (#J7178—$1.95)

☐ **THE NOSTALGIA QUIZ BOOK by Martin A. Gross.** A collection of over 1,500 memory-teasers on early movies, radio shows, comic books, swing bands, hit records, fads, ads, headlines, history, sports, slang and the way we lived from Prohibition to Only Yesterday! (#W7384—$1.50)

---

**THE NEW AMERICAN LIBRARY, INC.,**
P.O. Box 999, Bergenfield, New Jersey 07621

Please send me the SIGNET BOOKS I have checked above. I am enclosing $_____(check or money order—no currency or C.O.D.'s). Please include the list price plus 35¢ a copy to cover handling and mailing costs. (Prices and numbers are subject to change without notice.)

Name_____

Address_____

City_____State_____Zip Code_____
Allow at least 4 weeks for delivery

# THE SPORTS NOSTALGIA QUIZ BOOK #2

Zander Hollander
and
David Schulz

AN ASSOCIATED FEATURES BOOK

A SIGNET BOOK
NEW AMERICAN LIBRARY
TIMES MIRROR

NAL BOOKS ARE ALSO AVAILABLE AT DISCOUNTS IN BULK QUANTITY
FOR INDUSTRIAL OR SALES-PROMOTIONAL USE. FOR DETAILS, WRITE TO
PREMIUM MARKETING DIVISION, NEW AMERICAN LIBRARY, INC.,
1301 AVENUE OF THE AMERICAS, NEW YORK, NEW YORK 10019.

Copyright © 1977 by Associated Features, Inc.

All rights reserved

SIGNET TRADEMARK REG. U.S. PAT. OFF. AND FOREIGN COUNTRIES
REGISTERED TRADEMARK—MARCA REGISTRADA
HECHO EN CHICAGO, U.S.A.

SIGNET, SIGNET CLASSICS, MENTOR, PLUME AND MERIDIAN BOOKS
*are published by The New American Library, Inc.,*
*1301 Avenue of the Americas, New York, New York 10019.*

First Signet Printing, February, 1977

1 2 3 4 5 6 7 8 9

PRINTED IN THE UNITED STATES OF AMERICA

# Contents

## BASEBALL

1. Grand Slams  2
2. Oops!  3
3. Kid Stuff  4
4. True or False?  4
5. Diamond Throats  6
6. Big League Manager  7
7. Just Plain Bill  8
8. I Wuz Robbed  9
9. Break-Ups  9
10. Diamond MVPs  10
11. Attribution  11
12. Outside the Hall  11
13. Battery Mates  13
14. Walk to Fame  14
15. First-Year Phenoms  14
16. National League Sluggers  16
17. Alias  17
18. Double Play Combinations  17
19. 20 or Bust  18
20. Bonus Baby  19
21. Cy Young Winners  19
22. Crosstown Rivals  20
23. Thieves Afoot  21
24. Average Hitters  22
25. Complete the Outfield  23
26. RBI Men  24
27. Replacements  24
28. From the Fourth Estate  25
29. American League Club Marks  26
30. Gone, But Not Forgotten  27
31. National League Club Marks  27
32. Swinging for the Fences  28
33. Animals in Uniform  29
34. Rare Pitchers  30
35. Expansion  30
36. Starts and Finishes  32
37. Special Delivery  33
38. The Jones Boys  33
39. American League Sluggers  34

# FOOTBALL

40. Pardon My Slip  38
41. All-Star Game  39
42. Initial Reaction  41
43. Olympians on the Gridiron  41
44. Tom, Dick, and Harry  42
45. Outland Winner  43
46. Lettermen at the Mike  43
47. AAFC  44
48. Backfields  44
49. The Heisman  45
50. 1,000-Yarders  46
51. Pro Combo  46
52. Football Handles  47
53. Davis, Davis, Davis  48
54. A Guy Named Joe  49
55. Super Linebackers  50
56. Days of Yore  51
57. Granddaddy of the Bowls  52
58. Wiffle  54
59. Autumn Colors  55
60. No. 1  56
61. Post-War Football War  56
62. Names of WFL Fame  58
63. Big Ten Battles  58
64. Trophy Games  60
65. What's-His-Name Smith  60
66. Notable Bowls  61
67. Continental League  62
68. All-Star Quarterback  63
69. WFL: Lost League  64

# BASKETBALL

70. First Fives  66
71. Of Diamonds and Hardwood  67
72. NIT Crown  68
73. NBA MVP  69
74. Amateur Ball  70
75. Cleaning the Boards  70
76. Pro Firsts  71
77. For the Birds  72
78. A Helping Hand  72
79. Once in the NBA  74
80. Final Foe  75
81. ABA Match-Ups  76
82. All-Indian  77
83. Getting the Bounces  77
84. College Scorers  78
85. Old Homes  79

86. One of a Kind  79
87. AAU All-Stars  80
88. Fast Break  81
89. ABL Legacy  82

## SPORTS & MOVIES

90. Featured Performer  84
91. Stars and the Silver Screen  84
92. Play Acting  85
93. Made in Heaven  85
94. Cinema Subject  86
95. Sports in the Background  87

## BOXING

96. Dethroned  90
97. Champs from Abroad  90
98. It's All History  91
99. Monikers  92
100. In the Same Boat  92
101. Identity Change  93

## TENNIS

102. Racket Country  96
103. Campus Netmen  97
104. Women Aces  97

## OLYMPICS

105. Water Kings  100
106. Women Olympians  101
107. Mat Masters  101
108. Fisticuffs  102
109. Court Play  103
110. Running for Gold  104
111. Manning the Lifts  105
112. A Jump in the Water  105
113. On the Track  106
114. A Bevy of Babes  108
115. Gold Fields  109
116. Water Queens  110
117. Flags of All Nations  111

## HOCKEY

118. Iron Men  114
119. Adding Up  114
120. Penalty Shot  115
121. NHL Trophy  116

122. It's Still Detroit  117
123. Brothers  118
124. By the Numbers  118
125. Nicknames on Ice  119
126. Stanley Cup  120

## GOLF

127. Who Am I?  122
128. College Champs  124
129. Above Par  124

## BOWLING

130. Right Up Your Alley  128

## HORSE RACING

131. Long Shots  132
132. Around the Oval  133
133. Triple Crown  133

## AUTO RACING

134. Behind the Wheel  136
135. Sports Car Circuits  137

## MIXED BAG

136. Female Firsts  140
137. Breaking the Barrier  140
138. Speedboats  141
139. Railroad Men  142
140. Ignominy  143
141. Name Tags  144
142. Ring a Bell?  145
143. Food for Thought  146
144. Streaks  147
145. Stars of the 1940s  148
146. A Vicious Cycle  148
147. Trademarks  149
148. Wild Men  149
149. Schools for Sprinting  149
150. Stars of the 1960s  150
151. Numbers Game  151
152. On the Prowl  151
153. On Cue  152
154. NCAA Champs  153
156. ANSWERS

# BASEBALL

# 1. Grand Slams

**1.** Only two men have hit grand slam home runs in their first major league games. The first was Philadelphia pitcher Bill Duggleby in 1898. Who turned the trick 70 years later?

**2.** Only two National Leaguers have hit World Series homers with the bases full. Name them.

**3.** Which American League hurler is the only pitcher ever to hit a World Series grand slam?

**4.** A pitcher is the only man in National League history to hit two grand slams in one game. Name him.

**5.** No one has hit more than five grand slams in a single season. Name the two sluggers, one from each league, who share the major league mark.

**6.** The first pinch-hit grand slam was hit June 3, 1902 by Michael J. O'Neill of the St. Louis Cardinals. Who are the three men who share the major league mark by hitting three grand slams as pinch-hitters, all since World War II?

**7.** What Detroit pitcher served up four grand slam pitches during the 1959 season?

**8.** What American League hurler offered a record nine grand slam pitches during his career from 1948 to 1961?

**9.** Lou Gehrig holds the record for career grand slams with 23. Off what Philadelphia A's pitcher did he hit his 23rd and last, on August 20, 1938?

## 2. Oops!

*There is more than one way to get into the record book. Can you identify these diamond heroes who would probably prefer to be remembered for other feats?*

**1.** What Cy Young Award-winning pitcher once yielded a record 15 gopher balls in 1960?

**2.** Who is the Hall of Fame pitcher who shares a major league record of throwing 156 wild pitches in his American League career?

**3.** What National League pitcher, who posted 13 20-victory seasons, also led the league in fielding errors five times?

**4.** What Angel pitcher once served up home run pitches to four batters in a row?

**5.** What Boston Red Sox slugger established a major league mark by grounding into 32 double plays in a season?

**6.** What Hall of Famer committed more errors, 271, than any other outfielder?

**7.** What Pirate slugger racked up 12 straight seasons of 100 or more strikeouts?

**8.** Name the four American Leaguers, all since World War II, who have led the major leagues more than once in the "most double plays hit into" category.

**9.** Who is the Hall of Fame hurler who gave up a record 502 home runs during his career?

**10.** Mickey Mantle is the all-time strikeout king of major league baseball with 1,710. Who was the National League's top whiffer with 1,526?

**11.** Al Downing served up Henry Aaron's 715th career home run, but what Cincinnati pitcher gave Aaron No. 714, enabling him to tie Babe Ruth's mark?

## 3. Kid Stuff

**1.** What noted speedballer, at age 20, was the youngest pitcher to start and win a World Series game when he turned the trick in 1913?

**2.** Cincinnati's Joe Nuxhall was the youngest major leaguer at 15, but what 16-year-old pitcher was the youngest player in American League history when he came up with Philadelphia in 1943?

**3.** Who is the youngest man ever to win a batting title?

**4.** What Dodger is the youngest National Leaguer ever to lead the league in batting?

**5.** Who is the 20-year-old who was the youngest American Leaguer ever to lead the league in homers when he hit 32 in 1965?

**6.** When Fred Lynn was named MVP in 1975, he became the youngest player, at 23, to be so honored. What National Leaguer was previously the youngest MVP?

## 4. True or False?

**1.** Henry Aaron once hit four home runs in a game.

**2.** Roberto Clemente was the last triple crown winner in the National League.

**3.** Bob Feller never won a World Series game.

**4.** The St. Louis Browns never won a pennant.

**5.** Ty Cobb, Tris Speaker, and Zack Wheat once played in the same outfield for the A's.

**6.** There has never been a league leader with a batting average below .300.

**7.** The Giants have never beaten the Yankees in the World Series.

**8.** Babe Ruth was a unanimous choice for the Hall of Fame.

**9.** Frank Howard once hit 10 home runs in 20 consecutive official at-bats.

**10.** Ernie Banks never played in the minor leagues.

**11.** Walter Alston never played in a major league game.

**12.** Dick Littlefield played for ten different major league teams.

**13.** Milt Pappas won 100 games in each league.

**14.** The Cleveland Indians were once known as the Molly Maguires.

**15.** Bobo Holloman's no-hitter was his only major league victory.

**16.** Willie Mays never led the league in RBIs.

**17.** The Yankees never finished in last place.

**18.** Jim Thorpe played major league baseball.

**19.** No American League shortstop since Harvey Kuenn and Gil MacDougald in 1956 has had a .300 season batting average.

**20.** No National League pitcher has ever thrown an opening day no-hitter.

**21.** Lou Gehrig hit more than 500 homers in his career.

**22.** No World Series has gone five games without each team committing at least one error.

**23.** At least one no-hitter was pitched in Griffith Stadium, Washington, D.C.

**24.** The Boston Braves were once known as the Bees.

**25.** Babe Ruth hit three home runs in his last major league game.


# 5. Diamond Throats

*Hook up these broadcasters with the teams with which they have been most closely associated.*

1. Bert Wilson
2. Byron Saam
3. Earl Gillespie
4. Mel Allen
5. Waite Hoyt
6. Red Barber
7. Bob Elson
8. Arch McDonald
9. Jimmy Dudley
10. Ty Tyson
11. Rosey Rowswell
12. France Laux

a) Chicago White Sox
b) Detroit Tigers
c) New York Yankees
d) St. Louis Cardinals
e) Washington Senators
f) Chicago Cubs
g) Philadelphia Phillies
h) Cleveland Indians
i) Milwaukee Braves
j) Pittsburgh Pirates
k) Brooklyn Dodgers
l) Cincinnati Reds

## 6. Big League Manager

**1.** Who managed more major league games than anyone else, 2,960, without winning a pennant?

**2.** Name the skipper of the Philadelphia Whiz Kids.

**3.** Who are the only three men to manage pennant winners in each league?

**4.** Who was the manager of the Red Sox when they achieved their "Impossible Dream" in 1967?

**5.** The Braves won consecutives pennants in Milwaukee in 1957 and 1958. Name their manager.

**6.** In 1966, the Detroit Tigers had three different men at the helm. Who were they?

**7.** In 1955, for the first time in history, Brooklyn won a World Series. Name the pilot.

**8.** At the tail end of the 1914 season, a 23-year-old shortstop became the youngest manager in major league history. He was a manager only a month but stuck around the majors as a player for more than a decade. Name him.

**9.** The Philadelphia Athletics' Connie Mack, who held the position for 49 years, was easily the oldest manager the big leagues have ever seen at age 88. Who was the National League's oldest skipper at age 75?

**10.** What team hired the same man as manager for four different stints? Also name the manager.

**11.** Name the five different clubs managed by Jimmy Dykes.

# 7. Just Plain Bill

1. Name the Bill who is one of only a handful of pitchers who have had 20 victory seasons in each league.

2. Name the Bill who was the National League's last .400 hitter.

3. Who was the Bill, a real speed merchant, who was one of the top base stealers in the National League in the 1950s.

4. What Bill picked up nicknames like "Specs" and "Cricket" as an infielder before turning to managing in 1956?

5. Who was the Bill who was a mainstay alongside Al Kaline in the Detroit outfield before moving to Kansas City and Minnesota?

6. This Bill was a pitcher and wore uniform number 96. Name him.

7. Since 1950, Bills have been responsible for four no-hitters in the major leagues. Name them.

8. Who was the Bill, actually a Billy, who won 211 games during his 18-year career, appearing in World Series games with teams from each league?

9. What Bill made it into the Hall of Fame as an umpire?

10. Name the last Bill, one in each league, to win 20 games in one season.

11. There have been a couple of Willies and a Billy, but only one Bill who earned league Rookie of the Year honors. Name him.

**12.** Only two Bills have led the league in home runs. Name the men, one from each league, who did it.

**13.** The last time a pitching Bill led the majors in victories was 1938, the year he had a 22-9 record for Chicago. Name him.

**14.** Name the Bill, a pitcher for the Chicago Cubs, who struck out four men in one inning during a game in 1974.

**15.** Who was the Bill, also called Baby Doll, who had a .311 lifetime batting average playing between 1915 and 1927 with five different American League clubs?

# 8. I Wuz Robbed

*Great catches have been a part of baseball from the beginning. Identify the batters who were robbed of base hits in World Series games on spectacular plays by these fielders.*

1. Al Gionfriddo
2. Willie Mays
3. Brooks Robinson

# 9. Break-Ups

**1.** In the 1945 World Series, Chicago Cub pitcher Claude Passeau fashioned a one-hitter. What Tiger got the lone Detroit hit?

**2.** Pittsburgh's Harvey Haddix ran a perfect game into the 13th inning against the Milwaukee Braves in 1959. Who broke up the perfect game by reaching base on an error? Who later broke up the no-hitter?

**3.** When Johnny Vander Meer was fashioning his second consecutive no-hitter against the Brooklyn Dodgers in 1938, who was the last Dodger batter he faced?

**4.** Who broke up Floyd "Bill" Bevens' no-hit try in the 1947 World Series with a two-out double in the ninth inning?

**5.** When Sandy Koufax pitched his fourth career no-hitter, it was a perfect game against the Chicago Cubs in 1965. Cub pitcher Bob Hendley hurled a one-hitter against Koufax. What Dodger got the only hit of the game?

**6.** Who was the pinch-hitter who failed to break up Don Larsen's perfect game when he took a called third strike in the 1956 World Series?

## 10. Diamond MVPs

**1.** Modern baseball's Most Valuable Player awards date back to 1931. Who were the first two men to be honored by their respective leagues?

**2.** Who are the only two Braves to have been National League MVPs?

**3.** While there have been several repeat MVPs in the American League, only two National Leaguers were selected two years running. Name them.

**4.** Which American League teams have never had an MVP?

**5.** What five National League teams have never had a league MVP?

**6.** Who are the only Minnesota Twins to have been named MVP?

**7.** Only six second basemen, three in each league, have earned MVP honors. Name them.

**8.** Who is the only man to earn the MVP award in each league?

**9.** Who is the American Leaguer who is the only man to win MVP recognition with two different teams in the same league?

**10.** Who was the first black man to be named American League MVP?

# 11. Attribution

*Many baseball clichés were once original statements—at least that's what the sportswriters said when they wrote them. Identify the sources for these chestnuts.*

1. "Hit 'em where they ain't."
2. "Good field, no hit."
3. "It gets late early this time of year."
4. "They woulda had 'im at second, but he slud."
5. "Can't anybody here play this game?"
6. "It ain't nothin' till I call it."

# 12. Outside the Hall

*Identify these players who, despite their achievements, are not enshrined in baseball's Hall of Fame.*

**1.** A third baseman with more than 15 years in the American League, this non-member had a lifetime batting average of

.306, with high seasons of .340 and .343. He even won the league batting crown in 1949.

**2.** Another 15-year veteran, with playing time in both leagues, this non-member socked 359 home runs and drove in 1,337 runs while compiling a .312 batting average in a career that spanned the World War II years.

**3.** One of only two catchers to win the National League batting title, this non-member racked up a .306 lifetime average and was also on the receiving end of several no-hitters, handling eight 20-game winners in his 17-year career, mostly with Cincinnati.

**4.** In a career that stretched from 1939 to 1960, this outsider had high batting seasons of .353 (beating out Ted Williams for the title) and .333. In addition, this first baseman was also known as an exceptional fielder.

**5.** One of the few men to hit 500 home runs in a career, this non-member drove in 1,453 runs to be one of only 20 men in the history of the game to reach that level. He was a third baseman, which may explain it, since only three men at that position have been voted in.

**6.** This non-member hit 300 home runs and had a lifetime batting average of .320 during a 14-year career in which he also drove in more than 1,200 runs. He even led the league in stolen bases one season. Most of his career was spent with second-division National League clubs (several last-place finishers), but when he got into the World Series in 1935, he batted .333 for the Series.

## 13. Battery Mates

*The year was 1960, the last time the major leagues had only 16 teams. Match the top-winning pitchers for each club that season, in the left hand column, with the primary receivers, in the middle. Then put them on the correct team.*

| | | |
|---|---|---|
| 1. Bud Daley | A) Smokey Burgess | a) Baltimore Orioles |
| 2. Bill Monbouquette | B) Ed Bailey | b) Philadelphia Phillies |
| 3. Frank Lary | C) Del Crandall | c) Cincinnati Reds |
| 4. Chuck Stobbs | D) Russ Nixon | d) Los Angeles Dodgers |
| 5. Jim Perry | E) Hal Smith | e) Milwaukee Braves |
| 6. Billy Pierce | F) Lou Berberet | f) Kansas City A's |
| 7. Chuck Estrada | G) John Roseboro | g) Detroit Tigers |
| 8. Art Ditmar | H) Earl Battey | h) Cleveland Indians |
| 9. Robin Roberts | I) Bob Schmidt | i) Pittsburgh Pirates |
| 10. Glenn Hobbie | J) John Romano | j) Boston Red Sox |
| 11. Bob Purkey | K) Pete Daley | k) Washington Senators |
| 12. Sam Jones | L) Sherm Lollar | l) Chicago White Sox |
| 13. Don Drysdale | M) Moe Thacker | m) New York Yankees |
| 14. Ernie Broglio | N) Gus Triandos | n) Chicago Cubs |
| 15. Warren Spahn | O) Jimmie Coker | o) San Francisco Giants |
| 16. Vernon Law | P) Elston Howard | p) St. Louis Cardinals |

13

## 14. Walk to Fame

**1.** It happened at the Polo Grounds on July 23, 1944. A Chicago Cub batter was given an intentional walk with the bases full. Name him.

**2.** What American League slugger once played in 19 straight games during the 1938 season in which he received at least one base on balls each game?

**3.** What pesky-hitting National League second baseman walked 13 times during a 12-game streak in 1972?

**4.** Who holds the career record for most bases on balls?

**5.** The game is best remembered because Houston's Bob Watson scored major league baseball's one millionth run. But it was also the first game of a double header in which a record 42 walks were issued. Name the Astro and Giant pitchers who issued more than one walk that day.

## 15. First-Year Phenoms

**1.** Since the Rookie of the Year award began in 1947, four National League teams have not had a player selected for the honor. Name them.

**2.** Only five of the present American League teams have not had a league Rookie of the Year. Which are they?

**3.** Six first basemen, three in each league, have been named top rookies. Who are they?

**4.** What three catchers have won the rookie award?

**5.** Expansion came in 1961, but it wasn't until 1967 that a rookie on an expansion club was honored as Rookie of the Year. Who was he?

**6.** What Philadelphia A's hurler was the first pitcher to be named American League Rookie of the Year when he won in 1952?

**7.** Washington had consecutive rookie award winners in 1958 and 1959. Who were they?

**8.** The Dodgers have had the most winners of the rookie award, four in Brooklyn and three in Los Angeles. How many can you name?

**9.** As a rookie in 1954, Henry Aaron batted .280, hit 13 homers, and drove in 69 runs, but that wasn't good enough to win rookie recognition in the National League. Who beat him out?

**10.** Six Yankees have been named American League Rookie of the Year. Name them.

**11.** Who holds the record for most hits by a rookie, 223, set back in 1927?

**12.** What pitcher holds the distinction of being the oldest rookie since 1900 when he made his big league debut past the age of 40?

## 16. National League Sluggers

**1.** Only four National Leaguers have hit 50 or more homers in a season. Name them.

**2.** Since World War II, the lowest total to lead the National League in homers was 23. Who had that many, and in what year?

**3.** What National League batter was the first major leaguer to hit more than 20 home runs in a season when he slammed 24 in 1915?

**4.** What National League hitter rapped 475 home runs in his career yet never led the league in that department?

**5.** Three switch-hitters share the league record of twice hitting home runs from each side of the plate in the same game. Name the trio.

**6.** Name the last Dodger to lead the National League in homers.

**7.** Who holds the league record of hitting 30 or more home runs for nine straight seasons?

**8.** Who holds the National League mark for leading the league in homers, turning the trick seven times?

**9.** Rudy York holds the major league record with 18 home runs in a single calendar month. Who holds the National League record of 17?

**10.** What two senior circuit batters share the major league record of hitting five homers in a double header?

## 17. Alias

*Match the nicknames on the left with the appropriate team.*

1. Gashouse Gang
2. Whiz Kids
3. Murderers Row
4. Hitless Wonders
5. Baby Birds
6. Mustache Gang

a) Chicago White Sox
b) Baltimore Orioles
c) Oakland A's
d) St. Louis Cardinals
e) Philadelphia Phillies
f) New York Yankees


## 18. Double Play Combinations

*Tinker to Evers to Chance made better poetry than they did double plays, but there were those shortstops, second basemen, and first basemen who were formidable combinations. Match these.*

1. Crosetti to Lazzeri to
2. Jurges to Herman to
3. Rogell to Gehringer to
4. Kessenger to Beckert to
5. Barry to Collins to
6. Groat to Mazeroski to

a) McInnis
b) Stuart
c) Gehrig
d) Greenberg
e) Grimm
f) Banks

## 19. 20 or Bust

**1.** The last time one National League team had two pitchers who won 50 games between them was 1939. What was the team, and who were the pitchers?

**2.** In the last 50 years there have been only four pitchers who have won 20 games in a season in each league. Who are they?

**3.** In 1971, Baltimore had four 20-game winners and won the pennant. The 1920 Chicago White Sox also had four 20-game winners, but could do no better than finish in second place. Name the hurlers who toiled in vain.

**4.** When was the last time two American League pitchers on the same team won 50 games between them in a season?

**5.** Who was the National League's last 30-game winner? The American League's?

## 20. Bonus Baby

*The big, often six-figure contract for untried high school and college athletes was a phenomenon of the 1950s. Match these bonus babies with the clubs that signed them.*

1. Billy Joe Davidson
2. Bruce Gruber
3. Ted Kazanski
4. Paul Pettit
5. Danny Murphy
6. Bob Taylor
7. Bob Garibaldi
8. Dave Nicholson

a) San Francisco Giants
b) Milwaukee Braves
c) Cleveland Indians
d) Baltimore Orioles
e) Philadelphia Phillies
f) Pittsburgh Pirates
g) Philadelphia Phillies
h) Chicago Cubs

## 21. Cy Young Winners

**1.** The Cy Young Award is given annually to the best pitcher in each major league, but originally there was only one winner for the two leagues. Who was the initial recipient, in 1956?

**2.** Name the five men who have been honored more than once.

**3.** Of the present 14 American League teams, which five have not had a Cy Young winner?

**4.** Who is the only relief pitcher to win the trophy?

19

**5.** There are four National League teams which have never boasted a Cy Young winner. Which are they?

**6.** The Angels have had several 20-game winners since they began as an expansion team in 1961. Which one earned Cy Young recognition?

**7.** Only two Cy Young winners have had less than 20 victories in the year they were honored. Who are they?

**8.** Only once has there been a tie in the award voting. Who shared the American League honors in 1969?

**9.** After a decade of one winner for the major leagues, the voting was split in 1967 to have a winner from each league. Who were the first two winners under the new format?

**10.** Who is the only Chicago White Sox pitcher to receive the Cy Young Award?

# 22. Crosstown Rivals

*Of the six cities which were represented by a team in each major league, which of the following were never treated to an intra-city World Series?*

    a) St. Louis
    b) Philadelphia
    c) New York
    d) Boston
    e) Los Angeles
    f) Chicago

## 23. Thieves Afoot

**1.** Since 1953, only six men have led the National League in stolen bases. Name them.

**2.** Two players share the record with 14 stolen bases in World Series competition. Name the thieves, one from each league.

**3.** In this century, Philadelphia has had only three men who have led the National League in stolen bases. Name the 1932, 1941, and 1948 kings.

**4.** Who was the top American League base stealer nine years running in the 1950's and early '60's?

**5.** Who hold the record of having played in 1,206 consecutive games without getting caught stealing? Actually he stole only one base, and it was the only time he tried, in 1958.

**6.** Since World War II there have been three players who stole home in the World Series. Who are they?

**7.** Only once in the last 50 years has a player stolen home twice in one game. Name the American Leaguer who did it in 1958.

**8.** The record for most bases stolen in All-Star Games is six. Who holds it?

**9.** Only four players who played most of their career after 1950 have stolen 500 or more bases. Name them.

**10.** The 1962 Dodgers, led by Maury Wills, stole 198 bases. Wills accounted for 104 of these, but name the four other Dodgers who had 10 or more.

## 24. Average Hitters

**1.** The 1906 Chicago White Sox, known as the Hitless Wonders, won the American League pennant and World Series with a team batting average of .228. More than half a century later a National League team won the pennant and Series with an all-time National League pennant-winning low average of .242. Name the team.

**2.** The 1930 New York Giants established a post-1900 record by batting .319 for the season. Name the nine players who batted over .300 while playing in most of the team's games.

**3.** It was really a hitter's year in 1930 when the St. Louis Cardinals came up with 10 players who played in at least half the games and batted over .300. Name them.

**4.** In 1961, the Tigers led the American League in batting for a record 16th time in that league with only two .300 batters playing regularly. Who were they?

**5.** The 1968 Oakland A's led the American League with a team batting average of .240, the lowest ever for a league leader. Who was Oakland's top hitter with a .290 average?

**6.** The American League rapped out 14 hits in its 12-0 romp over the National League in the 1946 All-Star Game at Boston. Name the two players who got more than one hit.

**7.** The lowest batting average by any team in the last 50 years was the .214 recorded by the Yankees in 1968. Their leading hitter was an outfielder who batted .267. Name him.

**8.** What Detroit infielder holds the career batting average record in All-Star competition with 10 hits in 20 at-bats?

**9.** The lowest batting average for the winner of a seven-game World Series came in 1962 when the Yankees hit .199 against San Francisco. Who was the Yankee outfielder who outperformed his teammates with a .321 average?

**10.** The highest batting average by any World Series team was the .338 by the losing Yankees in 1960. Who were the team's big guns, batting .300 or better against the Pirates?

## 25. Complete the Outfield

**1.** When Roberto Clemente made his major league debut on April 17, 1955, he was in right field for the Pirates. Who was in the outfield with him that day?

**2.** Who played in the outfield with the M & M boys most of the time when Maris and Mantle were slugging homers for the Yankees in 1961?

**3.** What trio was the backbone of the St. Louis Cardinal outfield in the 1940s?

**4.** Name the outfield for Philadelphia's Whiz Kids of 1950.

**5.** The New York Yankee outfield of 1932 batted .319 and drove in 302 runs. Name this threesome.

**6.** When the Braves won consecutive National League pennants in 1957-58, they relied on five outfielders in the 14 World Series Games. Who were the five?

**7.** When Paul and Lloyd Waner were patrolling the outfield for Pittsburgh in the 1920s and 1930s, they had two men, each of whom played 500 or more games between them. Name the pair.

**8.** The Yankees won their fifth straight World Series in 1953 with what three outfielders playing every minute of every game?

**9.** Ty Cobb hit .401 for Detroit in 1921, and Harry Heilmann batted .403 the following season. Who was in the outfield with them?

**10.** Who was with Ted Williams in the Boston outfield in 1941 when the Splendid Splinter batted .406?

# 26. RBI Men

**1.** Only six men have driven in 150 or more runs in a single National League season. Name them.

**2.** Lou Gehrig, a first baseman, holds the American League record for most RBIs. Who holds the National League record for RBIs by a first baseman with 142 in one season?

**3.** Only one Chicago White Sox batter finished the season leading the American League in RBIs. Who was it?

**4.** The last time an RBI leader in either league finished with fewer than 100 was in 1920. Name the two National Leaguers who shared the crown with 94 that season.

**5.** The major league record for RBIs by a team in one season is 995 by the 1936 Yankees. Name the five players who had 100 or more for the Bronx Bombers that year.

# 27. Replacements

**1.** Who was the Orioles' third baseman before Brooks Robinson took over regular duty in 1958?

**2.** Wally Pipp was the Yankee first baseman before Lou Gehrig started his 2,130-game string. Who replaced Gehrig?

**3.** While Yogi Berra was playing behind the plate in virtually every game for the Yankees between 1948 and 1956, who spent most of the time on the bench waiting to replace him?

**4.** Who is the only man ever to pinch-hit for Ted Williams?

## 28. From the Fourth Estate

**1.** What *New York Times* sportswriter is credited with devising the first system for keeping score?

**2.** Who was the syndicated columnist who described a superior pitcher as a man who "could throw a lambchop past a wolf?"

**3.** Who wrote the poem "Casey at the Bat"?

**4.** Which pre-1900 Boston scribe is generally credited with being the first newspaperman to take baseball seriously?

**5.** Who was the one-time sports editor of the Cincinnati *Gazette* who became president of the American League?

**6.** Who penned the words immortalizing Joe Tinker, Johnny Evers, and Frank Chance?

**7.** Who was the one-time employee of the Hearst newspaper empire who became a National League president?

# 29. American League Club Marks

**1.** Luke Appling holds most of the Chicago White Sox career batting records, but he isn't even in the top ten in the club for lifetime home runs. Who is the all-time White Sox home run slugger?

**2.** Which Oriole holds the Baltimore team record with 141 runs batted in for a single season?

**3.** One man holds the single-season stolen base record for two different American League clubs. Who is he, and which are the clubs?

**4.** No one has more 1,000-RBI hitters than the Tigers. Name the eight men who reached that total with Detroit.

**5.** The Yankee team record for highest batting average in one season is .393. Who holds it?

**6.** What Boston batter hit safely in 34 straight games in 1949 to establish the Red Sox club mark?

**7.** Only three Indians hit 200 or more home runs playing with Cleveland. Who are they?

**8.** What seven men had .300-plus career batting averages with the Yankees?

**9.** Frank Howard holds most of the batting records in the brief history of the Washington/Texas franchise, but an infielder not known as a hitter owns the club career mark for triples. Name him.

**10.** Which six Minnesota batters rapped out 1,000 or more hits with the Twins?

## 30. Gone, But Not Forgotten

*Identify the city where these major league baseball parks were located.*

1. Polo Grounds
2. Forbes Field
3. Shibe Park
4. Briggs Stadium
5. Sportsman's Park
6. Crosley Field
7. Ebbets Field
8. Colt Stadium
9. Braves Field
10. Seals Stadium
11. Sicks Stadium
12. Griffith Stadium
13. Memorial Coliseum

## 31. National League Club Marks

**1.** One man holds the single-season batting average record for three different National League teams. Who is he, and which are the teams?

**2.** Another batter holds the single-season average record for two expansion teams. Name him and the teams.

**3.** Who holds the St. Louis Cardinal team record of 154 RBIs in one season?

**4.** Henry Aaron holds most of the Braves' career records, but one which eluded him was most triples. Who holds the team career mark of 103?

**5.** Likewise for the Giants, Willie Mays holds most of the club's lifetime marks. One notable exception is in RBIs, where somebody literally one-upped him by getting 1,860 to Willie's 1,859. Name the Giant leader.

**6.** Five Pittsburgh players have driven in 1,000 or more runs in their careers as Pirates. Name them.

**7.** Which of the Whiz Kids is Philadelphia's all-time leading home run hitter?

**8.** Who holds the Braves' team record of 224 hits in one season?

**9.** Although his name is usually remembered in connection with double plays, this Chicago Cub holds the team single-season stolen base mark with 67. Name him.

**10.** Stan Musial is far and away the leading home run hitter for the Cardinals with 475. Who ranks next with 255?

## 32. Swinging For The Fences

**1.** In 1953, for the first time in National League history, four players hit 40 or more home runs in the same season. Name them.

**2.** The 1973 Atlanta Braves were the first team to have three 40-home run hitters in one season. Identify them.

**3.** The record for home runs hit on the road is 30. Who set the record in 1953?

**4.** Only four men have hit World Series home runs for teams from both leagues. Name them.

**5.** What Red Sox player holds the American League record for most pinch-hit home runs in a season with five?

**6.** Who holds the major league record for pinch-hit home runs in a career with 18?

**7.** What three pitchers gave up three home runs apiece to Roger Maris during his 61-homer season?

## 33. Animals in Uniform

*Identify these baseball players who were or are often referred to in these bestial terms:*

1. Vulture
2. Moose
3. Goose
4. Rabbit
5. Spider
6. Ducky
7. King Kong
8. Silver Fox
9. Hawk
10. Mule
11. Penguin
12. Mudcat
13. Bear
14. Baby Bull
15. Red Rooster

## 34. Rare Pitchers

*Four of these men never pitched in a major league game. Name them.*

a) Henry Aaron
b) Stan Musial
c) Ted Williams
d) Rocky Colavito
e) Honus Wagner
f) Ralph Kiner
g) Roger Maris
h) Ty Cobb
i) Jimmy Dykes
j) Roy Sievers

## 35. Expansion

*For 60 years, major league baseball meant 16 clubs, eight in each league. Then came expansion.*

**1.** Which were baseball's 17th and 18th major league clubs?

**2.** Who were the first managers of those two teams?

**3.** When expansion came in 1961, who was the first player selected in the draft?

**4.** Who was the first player selected by the new Washington franchise?

**5.** When expansion came to the National League, it was in

Houston and New York. Name the managers of those two teams in their initial seasons.

**6.** Just as the Yankees provided the first two selections in the first American League expansion draft, so did one National League team provide the first two choices for the Mets and Colt 45s. Name the team.

**7.** Who were the first two National League draft choices?

**8.** Who were the last two National League draft choices for the 1962 expansion teams?

**9.** In the expansion drafts of 1961 and 1962, who was the only player to be selected each time?

**10.** Of the 88 players who were on those American League expansion teams in 1961, only three of them were around the majors 15 years later, at the end of the 1975 season. Name them.

**11.** There were 89 different players who wore New York Met and Houston Astro uniforms in 1962. Only two of them were still playing in major league uniforms 15 seasons later, in 1976. Who were they?

**12.** The second round of expansion came in 1969. What four teams were added? Who were their managers?

**13.** For the 1969 drafts, the Giants again provided a first round draft pick. Who was it?

**14.** Who was the National League's other first round pick in 1969?

**15.** Name the first selections by the two American League expansion teams in 1969.

**16.** Of the eight expansion teams, which was the first to achieve a .500 season?

**17.** Of the "second generation" expansion clubs, which was the first to win more games than it lost?

**18.** San Diego's last pick in 1969 was with the team for several years before he was traded back to Atlanta, the team from which he had been drafted. Name this outfielder.

**19.** Bill Stoneman, who pitched two no-hitters for Montreal in their early years, was drafted from what National League team by the Expos?

# 36. Starts and Finishes

**1.** Roberto Clemente finished his career with exactly 3,000 base hits. What New York Met pitcher issued Clemente his last hit?

**2.** What Chicago White Sox pitcher threw Mickey Mantle the first of his 536 career home runs in 1951?

**3.** Which is the only city to be continuously represented in the National League since 1875?

**4.** Lefty Grove, at age 40, finally achieved the 300th and last victory of his career, a 10-6 triumph over Cleveland in 1941. For which team was Grove pitching?

**5.** Nolan Ryan started striking out batters when he came up with the New York Mets in 1966. Who caught Ryan's first big league "K"?

**6.** World Series competition came to Yankee Stadium in 1923. What visiting Giant clouted the first Series home run in the Stadium?

**7.** Connie Mack Stadium (a/k/a Shibe Park) last saw a major league game in 1970. What Phillie got the last hit there?

**8.** Who served Ted Williams his first major league hit?

**9.** Hank Bauer holds the World Series record for consecutive-game hitting streak at 17. Who snapped it in 1958?

**10.** Who was the Minnesota pinch-hitter who was Nolan Ryan's record 383rd strikeout victim in 1973?

# 37. Special Delivery

*Some pitchers were identified with oddball pitches. Can you match these throwers with their deliveries?*

1. Rip Sewell
2. Hoyt Wilhelm
3. Lew Burdette
4. Elroy Face
5. Stu Miller

a) Junk ball
b) Fork ball
c) Eephus pitch
d) Knuckle ball
e) Spitball

# 38. The Jones Boys

**1.** Who was Philadelphia's Jones boy, also known as "Puddin' Head"?

**2.** Who was the utility Jones who saw World Series action with the 1946 Cardinals and the 1957 Braves?

**3.** Who was the Jones who picked up a couple of nicknames during his days with the Indians, Cubs, Cardinals, Giants, Tigers, and Orioles as a better than .500 pitcher (102 victories, 101 losses) during the 1950s and 1960s?

**4.** This Jones had cups of coffee with San Francisco and Cincinnati before becoming one of the Amazing Mets in 1962. Name him.

**5.** A colorful figure with a nickname to match, which Jones spent most of the 1960s with the Braves before moving to Cincinnati and Montreal?

**6.** An American Leaguer all his career, who was the Jones who spent six years infielding for Boston before going to Detroit and Texas?

**7.** A versatile bird, this Jones played several positions in his 853 games with Detroit between 1917 and 1925.

## 39. AL Sluggers

**1.** Only two players from the Chicago White Sox have led the American League in home runs. Who are they?

**2.** Name the first New York player to lead the American League in homers. Then name the last.

**3.** Since 1950, the fewest number of home runs hit by a team in one season was 50 by Washington in 1952, yet three Senators hit 10 or more homers that year. Name them.

**4.** What slugger hit 399 career homers in the American League yet never led the league nor even finished in the runner-up spot in that department?

**5.** Who was the first Washington Senator to lead the league in home runs?

**6.** Only five players have hit 50 or more home runs in a single American League season. Name them.

**7.** Since Babe Ruth was the first American League slugger to hit more than 20 homers in a season (with 29 in 1919) what is the fewest number hit by a league leader?

**8.** What is the most home runs hit by a player who failed to lead the league?

**9.** Who was the first player with an expansion club to lead the American League in home runs?

**10.** When the Yankees set a major league record of 240 home runs in 1961, Maris and Mantle led the way. Nevertheless, there were four teammates who slammed 20 or more. Who were they?

# FOOTBALL

## 40. Pardon My Slip

*Record books keep track of bad performances as well as good ones. Identify these men by their football errors.*

1. What Houston quarterback set the record in 1962 by throwing 42 interceptions over the course of the season?

2. Who was the Dallas Cowboy kicker who missed a field goal only to have Philadelphia's Al Nelson run it back 101 yards for a touchdown on September 26, 1971?

3. Another Houston quarterback holds the record for most fumbles in a season, bobbling the ball 17 times in 1973. Name him.

4. Who was the Kansas City quarterback who fumbled seven times in a game against San Diego, November 15, 1964?

5. What Green Bay running back fumbled, allowing Oakland's Jack Tatum to scoop up the ball and return it 104 yards for a touchdown?

6. The last time a quarterback had as many as seven passes intercepted in a game was December 12, 1965. Name the Steeler thrower thus victimized by the Eagles.

7. What quarterback holds the career record for fumbles?

8. Three quarterbacks share the mark for fumbling four times in a game, but each time recovering them. A Brown did it in 1953, a Cardinal in 1961, and a Ram in 1969. Identify the fumblers.

9. Pittsburgh passers were tackled a record 12 times by Dallas Cowboy defenders on November 20, 1966. Who were the three frustrated Steeler throwers?

**10.** Green Bay picked off a record nine Detroit passes on October 24, 1943. What Lion quarterback contributed seven of the interceptions?

**11.** The Giants' Erich Barnes tied a league record with a 102-yard return of an intercepted pass on October 22, 1961. Who was the Dallas quarterback who threw the pass?

**12.** Only one man has fumbled three times in one Super Bowl game. Name the quarterback who did it.

**13.** Four quarterbacks have thrown three interceptions in a Super Bowl game, all of them on losing teams. Name them.

## 41. All-Star Game

**1.** The annual game between the NFL champion and the College All-Stars began in 1934, but it wasn't until two years later, after a 0-0 tie and 5-0 defeat in the first two games, that the collegians scored their first points, in a 7-7 tie against the Detroit Lions. What University of Minnesota running back scored the touchdown?

**2.** The last time the All-Stars defeated the pros was 1963, when Wisconsin quarterback Ron VanderKelen engineered a 20-17 upset of the Green Bay Packers. VanderKelen was the hero, but who was his Badger teammate who scored the last TD of the game to give the collegians the victory?

**3.** The Detroit Lions were thumped 35-19 by the All-Stars in 1958 as Bobby Layne threw five interceptions. What Texas A&M placekicker, later an NFL star, was the game's leading scorer with four field goals and three extra points?

**4.** SMU's Doak Walker and COP's Eddie LeBaron were in the backfield, while Minnesota's Gordie Soltau was playing end and kicking points as the Stars upended the Philadelphia

Eagles 17-7 in 1950, but it was a North Carolina runner who was the game MVP. Name him.

5. The 1943 contest was played at Northwestern's Dyche Stadium in Evanston, and the All-Stars were loaded with Big Ten stars such as Pete Pihos of Indiana and Otto Graham of Northwestern. It was, however, a fullback from Wisconsin who scored two TDs and a pair of extra points to lead the collegians to a 27-7 rout of the Redskins. Name that Badger who was to become a future star in the NFL.

6. After losing four straight games, the All-Stars got back on the winning track with a 30-27 squeaker over the Cleveland Browns in 1955. Name the Ohio State placekicker whose three field goals and two PATs made the difference.

7. A Wisconsin running back romped 68 yards for one score and hit pay dirt again on the receiving end of a 38-yard pass, the only two TDs scored in the All-Stars' 16-0 rout of the LA Rams in 1946. Name this Badger who would later play for those same Rams.

8. The closest the All-Stars have come to winning in the last decade was 1969, when Joe Namath and the Jets escaped with a 26-24 victory. What collegiate quarterback was selected the game MVP?

## 42. Initial Reaction

*Whatever their given names were, some football players were best known to fans by their initials. Identify these lettermen.*

1. Y.A.
2. R.C.
3. E.J.
4. W.K.
5. L.G.
6. J.C.
7. J.R.
8. J.D.
9. L.C.

## 43. Olympians on the Gridiron

**1.** Who is the Florida A&M sprinter who won gold medals at Tokyo in 1964 and played in the Super Bowl VI eight years later?

**2.** Name the Syracuse University quartermiler who earned Olympic gold in 1928 before turning pro with the NFL's Staten Island Stapletons in 1930.

**3.** Who was the former Olympic decathlon champion who was wearing a Giant uniform when the NFL came to New York in 1925?

**4.** Name the 1956 decathlon winner at Melbourne from Indiana University who played running back with the Cleveland Browns in 1957.

**5.** An Ohio Stater won a pair of gold medals—in the 400-meter hurdles and 1600-meter relay in Rome in 1960—before playing briefly as a wide receiver with the Detroit Lions. Name him.

**6.** What Kent State sprinter earned a gold medal as a member of the 400-meter relay team at Munich in 1972 before becoming a pro football player with the Atlanta Falcons?

## 44. Tom, Dick and Harry

**1.** Who is the Tom who holds the NFL record with a 63-yard field goal for the New Orleans Saints against the Detroit Lions?

**2.** What quarterback named Harry was a bonus draft pick by the Washington Redskins in 1948?

**3.** Who is the Dick who set a still-standing NFL record with 14 pass interceptions in 1952?

**4.** Only two Toms have ever led the NFL in passing, one playing for Cleveland in 1957 and one with Philadelphia in 1948. Identify them.

**5.** Who is the only gridder named Dick to put together two 1,000-yard seasons as an NFL running back?

**6.** Name the Tom who led the NFL in pass-receiving three straight years, 1948-50.

**7.** Who was the player named Dick who set Washington team records as a running back when he scored 4 TDs and 24 points against the Dallas Cowboys in 1961?

**8.** Name the former major league baseball player named Tom who was a defensive halfback on Green Bay's two Super Bowl teams.

**9.** Name the Harry who was a ball-carrying mainstay of the Cleveland Brown title teams of the early 1950s.

## 45. Outland Winner

*Which of these Texas Longhorns did not win the Outland Trophy as the nation's outstanding interior lineman?*

    a) Tommy Nobis
    b) Scott Appleton
    c) Jerry Sisemore

## 46. Lettermen at the Mike

*These men have all been network sportscasters, but before they were on the air, they played college football. Identify the schools they attended.*

| | | |
|---|---|---|
| 1. Pat Summerall | | a) Minnesota |
| 2. Kyle Rote | | b) Northwestern |
| 3. Alex Karras | | c) Syracuse |
| 4. Fran Tarkenton | | d) Michigan |
| 5. Frank Gifford | | e) Iowa |
| 6. Alex Hawkins | | f) South Carolina |
| 7. Bud Wilkinson | | g) Colorado |
| 8. Irv Cross | | h) Duke |
| 9. Paul Christman | | i) Georgia |
| 10. Fred Williamson | | j) Southern California |
| 11. Al DeRogatis | | k) Missouri |
| 12. Duffy Daugherty | | l) Arkansas |
| 13. Tom Brookshier | | m) Southern Methodist |
| 14. Tom Harmon | | n) Northwestern |

## 47. AAFC

*Identify by nickname, the All-America Football Conference franchise that was located in the following cities.*

1. Buffalo
2. Cleveland
3. Baltimore
4. Brooklyn
5. Los Angeles
6. San Francisco
7. Chicago
8. Miami
9. New York

## 48. Backfields

1. Although he played quite a bit, Elmer Angsman was not a starter in Jim Conzelman's "Dream Backfield" for the 1947 Chicago Cardinals. Who were the four starters?

2. What running combination of the last decade was known as Butch Cassidy and the Sundance Kid?

3. Who was the fourth "horseman" in Notre Dame's fabled backfield with quarterback Harry Stuhldreher, fullback Elmer Layden, and "Sleepy" Jim Crowley at one halfback?

4. When Charley Johnson left New Mexico State in 1961, there were two Aggies in the backfield with him who made the pros as running backs. Name them.

**5.** The 1956 Illinois team had four backfield men who went on to notable careers as professionals. With halfbacks like Bobby Mitchell and Abe Woodson, and Ray Nitschke at fullback, who was the sophomore who played quarterback part time?

**6.** John Hadl was a long-time pro from Kansas, but two of his Jayhawk backfield mates in the early 1960s also had pro careers, although somewhat briefer. Name them.

**7.** The Green Bay Packers already had Jimmy Taylor and Paul Hornung as running backs on a championship team, yet the "war" with the AFL forced Vince Lombardi to shell out big bucks for a pair of collegiate running backs immediately dubbed the "Gold Dust Twins." Name this pair.

**8.** It took place on December 28, 1958 at Yankee Shadium—the NFL championship game. The teams? The Colts and the Giants. It went into sudden-death overtime, the first ever in the NFL, and when it was over, the Colts had won, 23-17. Who made up the Colt backfield in what has been called "the greatest NFL title game in history."

# 49. The Heisman

*Which of these pro football stars was the only one to have won college football's Heisman Trophy?*

a) Alan Ameche
b) Sammy Baugh
c) Jimmy Brown

## 50. 1,000-Yarders

*Which three of these college running backs put together three consecutive 1,000-yard seasons?*

   a) O. J. Simpson, Southern California
   b) Chris Gilbert, Texas
   c) Ron Johnson, Michigan
   d) Ed Marinaro, Cornell
   e) Woody Green, Arizona State
   f) Greg Pruitt, Oklahoma

## 51. Pro Combo

*Match the nicknames for teams or units of pro teams with the clubs they played for.*

1. Monsters of the Midway
2. Fearsome Foursome
3. No-Name Defense
4. Doomsday Defense
5. Purple Gang

   a) Miami Dolphins
   b) Minnesota Vikings
   c) Chicago Bears
   d) Los Angeles Rams
   e) Dallas Cowboys

## 52. Football Handles

*Fill in the blanks with the name by which these pro players were familiarly known.*

1. Robert Lee _____ Huff
2. Alphonse _____ Leemans
3. Robert Hardy _____ Turner
4. Edward _____ McDaniel
5. Christian Adolph _____ Jurgensen III
6. Carlton Chester _____ Gilchrist
7. Bryan _____ Starr
8. Junious _____ Buchanan
9. Earl _____ Lambeau
10. Marlin _____ Harder
11. Frank _____ Kilroy
12. Fletcher _____ Perry
13. Raymond _____ McLean
14. John _____ Driscoll
15. Floyd _____ Reid
16. Lance _____ Alworth
17. Palmer _____ Retzlaff
18. George _____ Summerall
19. George _____ Poole
20. Loris _____ Baker
21. Ewell _____ Walker
22. Edmund _____ Bratkowski

## 53. Davis, Davis, Davis

**1.** Who was the Davis who set several collegiate rushing and scoring records in the 1940s before playing with the Los Angeles Rams in 1950-51?

**2.** This Davis was an all-league defensive back who led the NFL in interceptions while playing with the Baltimore Colts in 1957. Name him.

**3.** Who was the 1961 All-American from Syracuse named Davis who was drafted by the Washington Redskins but never got to play because he had leukemia?

**4.** Name the Davis who was the only man to win the 400-meter hurdle events in two successive Olympics who later played professional football with the Detroit Lions.

**5.** Who was the Alabama Davis who played tackle for the Redskins and Bears in the 1940s, earning all-league recognition along the way.

**6.** Who was the Davis playing defensive back for Cleveland in 1968 who intercepted passes in seven straight games?

**7.** What San Francisco kicker named Davis has the second-highest lifetime punting average with 44.68 yards per kick in the NFL between 1959 and 1969?

**8.** Name the Davis who was let go by the Cleveland Browns and then became an anchor on the defensive line of Green Bay's Super Bowl teams.

## 54. A Guy Named Joe

1. Although everybody called him Joe, his real name was Fletcher and he was an all-star running back for the 49ers and the Colts. Name him.

2. Who was the linebacking Joe who recovered 22 opponents' fumbles for the Chicago Bears between 1955 and 1966?

3. Name the Joe who was a standout in the early days of the NFL after playing with Jim Thorpe at Carlisle and at Georgia Tech. He is in the Hall of Fame for his feats with such pro teams as the Canton Bulldogs, Rock Island Independents, Kansas City Cowboys, and New York Giants between 1918 and 1927.

4. Name the Joe from Minnesota who tied a league record by throwing seven TD passes against the Colts on September 28, 1969.

5. Who was the Joe from West Virginia who was an all-league tackle for the Chicago Bears between 1936 and 1946?

6. Name the Joe in the NFL Hall of Fame who was a linebacker for the Detroit Lions from 1953 to 1965 and later coached the team.

7. Who is the Joe who tied a league standard at the time when he returned eight punts in a single game for San Francisco against Detroit, October 16, 1955?

8. Who is the only Joe ever to pass for 400 or more yards in an NFL game, a feat he accomplished four times?

9. Name the Green Bay defensive back called Joe who intercepted a championship-game record three passes against the New York Giants in 1944.

10. What Joe from VMI was a standout running back and punter for the Philadelphia Eagles from 1946 to 1950?

## 55. Super Linebackers

**1.** The starting linebacking trio for the Green Bay Packers was the same in the first two Super Bowls. Name the threesome.

**2.** Pittsburgh limited the Minnesota Vikings to a record low 119 yards in total offense in Super Bowl IX. Name the starting Steeler linebackers.

**3.** Super Bowl III was the year Joe Namath guaranteed the Jets would win it, but who were the three starting linebackers who helped Joe look good?

**4.** Dallas' Doomsday Defense dominated Super Bowl VI. Name the starting linebackers for the Cowboys.

**5.** Everyone remembers Jim O'Brien's field goal winning Super Bowl V, but can you name the Colts who began the game at linebacker?

## 56. Days of Yore

*Many different cities have been represented in the NFL in the league's more than half a century of operation, and teams have come and gone. Match these franchises with their nicknames.*

1. Staten Island
2. Duluth
3. Akron
4. Frankford
5. Boston
6. Hammond
7. Brooklyn
8. Oorang (Marion, O.)
9. Buffalo
10. Minneapolis
11. Louisville
12. New York
13. Columbus
14. Pottsville
15. Kansas City
16. Portsmouth
17. Canton
18. Rochester
19. Detroit
20. New York
21. Dayton
22. Racine
23. Milwaukee
24. Providence
25. Cincinnati
26. Hartford
27. Dallas
28. St. Louis
29. Cleveland

aa) Legions
bb) Colonels
cc) Maroons
a) Indians
b) Rams
c) Tigers
d) Bulldogs
e) Bulldogs
f) Badgers
g) Blues
h) Stapletons
i) Steels
j) Panthers
k) Steamrollers
l) Texans
m) Eskimos
n) Gunners
o) Reds
p) Yellowjackets
q) Redskins
r) Pros
s) Bisons
t) Yankees
u) Spartans
v) Kodaks
w) Dodgers
x) Marines
y) Cowboys
z) Triangles

## 57. Granddaddy of the Bowls

**1.** The Rose Bowl began as an East-West contest between Michigan and Stanford in 1902. In all the games played since then, which are the only two Big Ten teams to have played in the Bowl and not won?

**2.** Who was the Notre Damer who established a record by returning two intercepted passes for a total of 148 yards in the 1925 game?

**3.** Three Rose Bowls have ended in ties. Match the teams who played in them:

    A) Washington    a) Alabama
    B) California     b) Navy
    C) Stanford      c) Washington & Jefferson

**4.** The most yards gained on receptions by a pass receiver was 164 in the 1935 game. Who was this Alabama end?

**5.** Name the only Southwestern team to play in the Rose Bowl, in 1936.

**6.** The longest run from scrimmage was an 84-yard scamper by what Michigan runner against Oregon State in 1965?

**7.** Which was the last team from neither the Big Ten nor the West Coast to play in the Rose Bowl?

**8.** The Mare Island Marines won the 1918 Rose Bowl by defeating Camp Lewis, 19-7. The following year the Great Lakes Naval Station whipped the Marines, 17-0. Name the former Illinois star, future New York Yankee baseballer, and Chicago Bear footballer who was on the Navy team.

**9.** What was the final score of the first game in the present Rose Bowl Stadium, on January 1, 1923?

**10.** What Southern California quarterback threw a record four TD passes in 1963?

**11.** Which Big Ten teams have played in more than one Rose Bowl and won every time?

**12.** What team has lost more Rose Bowl games, six, than any other team?

**13.** What Wisconsin quarterback set the single-game total offense record with 406 yards in 1963?

**14.** An all-time record 100,963 fans turned out for the 1950 Rose Bowl. What two teams played, and what was the final score?

**15.** The last time a defensive man was named outstanding player of the game was in 1967 when what Purdue Boilermaker was so honored?

**16.** What two players from San Francisco Bay area colleges share the Rose Bowl record with 34 rushing attempts each, one in 1925 the other in 1938?

**17.** In the 1971 affair, a Stanford placekicker booted a record 48-yard field goal. Name him.

**18.** The biggest rout in Rose Bowl history was 49-0, and the same team accomplished this twice. Name the team and its beaten foes.

**19.** The most yards gained rushing in a single game was 194 by what Iowa halfback in 1959?

**20.** What Wisconsin Badger hauled in 11 passes in 1963, setting a Rose Bowl mark?

## 58. Wiffle

*The World Football League, or "wiffle" as some people called it, is already a memory, although it wasn't born until 1973. How much do you remember about it? Match these WFL towns and the team nicknames.*

1. New York
2. Chicago
3. Charlotte
4. Florida
5. Birmingham
6. Memphis
7. Detroit
8. Honolulu
9. Houston
10. Shreveport
11. Jacksonville
12. Philadelphia
13. Portland
14. Southern California
15. Chicago
16. San Antonio
17. Jacksonville
18. Birmingham
19. Portland
20. Memphis

a) Blazers
b) Wheels
c) Sharks
d) Storm
e) Express
f) Hornets
g) Bell
h) Wind
i) Fire
j) Americans
k) Southmen
l) Hawaiians
m) Texans
n) Steamer
o) Thunder
p) Stars
q) Grizzlies
r) Wings
s) Sun
t) Vulcans

## 59. Autumn Colors

*A college football game is a colorful event, and some of the schools include color as part of the team nickname. Fill in the blanks with the appropriate color.*

1. Alabama _____ Tide
2. California _____ Bears
3. Rutgers _____ Knights
4. Texas Tech _____ Raiders
5. Delaware _____ Hens
6. Mississippi State _____
7. Dartmouth Big _____
8. Middle Tennessee _____ Raiders
9. Maine _____ Bears
10. Tulane _____ Wave
11. Duke _____ Devils
12. Syracuse _____-men
13. Kent State _____ Flashes
14. Cornell Big _____
15. Hawaii _____

## 60. No. 1

*Half of these colleges had football teams which were considered national champions in the last 50 years. Name them.*

a) Duke
b) Pittsburgh
c) Southern Methodist
d) Syracuse
e) Iowa
f) Navy
g) Minnesota
h) Miami (Fla.)
i) Fordham
j) Maryland

## 61. Post-War Football War

*The All-America Football Conference was founded in 1946, lasted four seasons, and waged a full-scale war with the established National Football League. How much do you remember about the AAFC?*

**1.** Sports luminaries were brought into the league's front office. What former Notre Dame great was the first president and commissioner of the league?

**2.** The widow of what baseball star was the league's first secretary?

**3.** Cleveland's Otto Graham wore the passing crown every season, although in 1946 he had to share it with which Brooklyn quarterback?

**4.** What New York running back set the single-season rushing mark with 1,432 yards in 14 games during the 1947 season?

**5.** Cleveland won all four AAFC championship games. Name the loser in each.

**6.** What San Francisco runner led the league in ground-gaining in its final season of 1949?

**7.** The league mark of 15 field goals in one season was set by what Los Angeles kicker?

**8.** What two Cleveland ends were the only pass catchers ever to lead the AAFC in receiving?

**9.** The scoring championship went to a different player each year: three runners and a kicker. Name this quartet.

**10.** Which nine of these players played in the AAFC?

    a) Y. A. Tittle
    b) Kyle Rote
    c) Bob Waterfield
    d) Buddy Young
    e) Marion Motley
    f) Bobby Layne
    g) Sid Luckman
    h) George Ratterman
    i) Barney Poole
    j) Paul Christman
    k) Jesse Freitas
    l) Ray Renfro
    m) Abe Gibron
    n) Elroy Hirsch
    o) Frank Sinkwich

## 62. Names of WFL Fame

*Hook up these pro footballers with the teams they played with in the World Football League.*

1. Larry Csonka
2. John Huarte
3. George Mira
4. Gerry Philbin
5. King Corcoran
6. Norris Weese
7. James McAlister
8. Virgil Carter
9. Rufus Ferguson
10. Jim Nance
11. Bob Davis
12. Alvin Wyatt
13. Jon Henderson

a) Jacksonville Sharks
b) Shreveport Steamer
c) Chicago Fire
d) Memphis Grizzlies
e) Florida Blazers
f) Portland Storm
g) Memphis Southmen
h) Detroit Wheels
i) Birmingham Americans
j) Philadelphia Bell
k) Southern California Sun
l) N.Y. Stars, Charlotte Hornets
m) Hawaiians

## 63. Big Ten Battles

*The Big Ten started life as the Intercollegiate Conference of Faculty Representatives in 1896, and no other collegiate athletic league has had as long a tradition of top-level football competition.*

1. Name the 11 schools which at one time or another have been members of the league popularly referred to as the "Western Conference" or the Big Ten.

2. What Michigan Wolverine set a pre-World War II career

scoring record in the Big Ten with 237 points on 33 TDs, 33 PATs, and two field goals?

**3.** What Purdue passer holds the Big Ten single-season records for total offense, most passes attempted and completed, and most touchdown passes?

**4.** During the 1960s, nine conference schools won or shared the league championship. Which was the only team that missed all the fun?

**5.** The last time the University of Chicago had an All-Big Ten player, he was also the Heisman Trophy winner. Name the Maroon quarterback who achieved the honor in 1935.

**6.** The longest forward pass in Big Ten history came on November 12, 1955, for Purdue against Northwestern. Name the future pro stars who combined on the 95-yard scoring pass for the Boilermakers.

**7.** Who was the Michigan State scatback who established a national record with 350 yards rushing against Purdue on October 30, 1971?

**8.** The record for most points in a league game is 30, set by Red Grange in 1924. What Michigan runner tied this mark against Wisconsin in 1968?

**9.** What Northwestern receiver established a conference mark by gaining 226 yards on nine receptions against Michigan State on November 25, 1972?

**10.** The all-time career punting average (post drop-kick era) is 40.4 yards on 111 punts by what Wisconsin Badger who made a name for himself in the pros as a placekicker?

**11.** Who is the Michigan receiver who set league marks with 698 yards gained on 50 catches in 1966?

## 64. Trophy Games

*Traditional games between college teams often have a trophy, significant or otherwise, at stake. Match these teams and the prize they have played for.*

1. Wisconsin vs. Minnesota
2. DePauw vs. Wabash
3. Michigan vs. Notre Dame
4. North Dakota vs. North Dakota State
5. Temple vs. Bucknell
6. Mississippi vs. Miss. State

a) Old Shoe
b) Golden Egg
c) Paul Bunyon Axe
d) Megaphone Trophy
e) Manon Bell
f) Nickel Trophy

## 65. What's-His-Name Smith

1. Who was the defensive lineman with Baltimore and Oakland with Super Bowl experience who was better known by his nickname than his given moniker, Charles Aaron Smith?

2. Name the Smith who was an all-league tackle and placekicker with the Green Bay championship teams of the 1930s.

3. Who was the Smith, playing for Detroit against the Chicago Bears, who established a league mark by returning an intercepted pass 102 yards for a TD in 1949?

4. This Smith was a pretty good receiver with Pittsburgh, but one Monday, on national TV, he was all alone and running for a TD when he raised the ball over his head in triumph,

fumbled the ball out of the end zone and wound up with no touchdown and, shortly afterward, a ticket to Houston.

**5.** Who is the Smith who shares an NFL record after his 106-yard return of a kickoff for the Kansas City Chiefs against Denver in 1967?

**6.** Name the Smith who attended Northwestern Louisiana before becoming one of the best tight ends in the NFL, playing his entire career with the same club.

**7.** Who was the Smith who was an all-league performer at end and placekicker for the Chicago Cardinals in the 1930s?

**8.** Who was the 14-year offensive line veteran from Arkansas, named Smith, who retired after the Colts won Super Bowl V, saying, "What can I possibly do after this?"

## 66. Notable Bowls

*There have been some unforgettable football games played on New Year's Days past, and just the final score is enough to evoke memories of these games. Match the winners on the left with their foes.*

1. Southern California 7
2. Texas 21
3. Mississippi 21
4. Illinois 40
5. Oklahoma 7
6. Boston College 19
7. Southern Methodist 21
8. Georgia 20
9. Washington 17
10. Alabama 34

a) North Carolina 10 (1947 Sugar)
b) Tennessee 13 (1941 Sugar)
c) Wisconsin 0 (1953 Rose)
d) Nebraska 7 (1967 Sugar)
e) Alabama 17 (1965 Orange)
f) Minnesota 7 (1961 Rose)
g) LSU 0 (1960 Sugar)
h) Stanford 7 (1952 Rose)
i) Maryland 0 (1954 Orange)
j) Oregon 13 (1948 Cotton)

## 67. Continental League

*The Continental League was a minor league with unfulfilled big league aspirations in the 1960's, but it served as a stepping stone for a few players enroute the NFL. Match these Continental League teams with their appropriate nicknames.*

1. Hartford
2. Orlando
3. Toronto
4. Montreal
5. Wheeling
6. Charleston
7. Norfolk
8. Richmond
9. Brooklyn
10. Alabama
11. Michigan

a) Rockets
b) Rebels
c) Hawks
d) Charter Oaks
e) Rifles
f) Arrows
g) Panthers
h) Dodgers
i) Beavers
j) Neptunes
k) Ironmen

# 68. All-Star Quarterback

*The men on the left were quarterbacks who played in the annual All-Star Game in Chicago. Match them with the colleges where they played varsity ball.*

1. Lamar McHan
2. Pete Beathard
3. Jack Scarbath
4. Arnie Tucker
5. Lou Saban
6. Craig Morton
7. Bill Anderson
8. Gary Lane
9. Norm Van Brocklin
10. Jack Mitchell
11. Zeke Bratkowski
12. Irv Kupcinet
13. Billy Wade
14. Fran Naugle
15. Terry Baker
16. Don Meredith
17. Bob Timberlake
18. Greg Landry
19. John Brodie
20. Jerry Reichow
21. Norm Snead
22. George Mira
23. Sammy Baugh
24. Steve Spurrier
25. Steve Sloan
26. Vito Parilli
27. Adrian Burke
28. Jim Ninowski
29. Ed Sharockman
30. Tommy O'Connell
31. Angelo Bertelli
32. Phil Nugent
33. Bobby Layne

a) Maryland
b) Indiana
c) Tulsa
d) Oregon
e) Georgia
f) Vanderbilt
g) Oregon State
h) Michigan
i) Massachusetts
j) Iowa
k) Texas Christian
l) Florida
m) Alabama
n) Baylor
o) Pittsburgh
p) Notre Dame
q) Texas
r) Arkansas
s) Southern California
t) Army
u) Tulane
v) Illinois
w) North Dakota
x) Nebraska
y) Southern Methodist
z) Stanford
aa) Wake Forest
bb) Miami (Fla.)
cc) Michigan State
dd) California
ee) Missouri
ff) Oklahoma
gg) Kentucky

## 69. WFL: Lost League

**1.** Where were Larry Csonka, Jim Kiick, and Paul Warfield going to play before owner John Bassett moved his team to Memphis and renamed them the Southmen?

**2.** Even before Csonka, Kiick, and Warfield got to Memphis, the Southmen had the best offensive unit in the WFL in 1974. Name the three runners who ranked among the top ten in the league.

**3.** What did the WFL call its point-after-touchdown play?

**4.** Who was Portland's 28-year-old back-up quarterback who was named head coach halfway through the team's first season?

**5.** What was the unusual measuring device called that was used to check first-down yardage?

**6.** What was the final score of the first World Bowl, the league's championship game, in 1974?

**7.** What three men shared Most Valuable Player honors for the initial season?

**8.** What Florida Blazer was the WFL Defensive Player of the Year in 1974?

**9.** Who were the two television announcers broadcasting the nationally televised WFL games?

**10.** Who was the Florida Blazer who led the league in rushing its first season?

**11.** Who was the league's leading rusher (1,200 yards) and scorer (16 TDs) when the WFL collapsed in mid-1975?

# BASKETBALL

## 70. First Fives

**1.** Who were the five starters for the Lakers when they won their first championship in 1952?

**2.** The Knicks captured their first NBA title in 1970 with what starting line-up in the final game against Los Angeles?

**3.** In 1958, the St. Louis Hawks were the last team to win a championship before Boston ran off its string of eight straight crowns. Who were the Hawk regulars that season?

**4.** Boston's first championship with Bill Russell in the line-up came in 1957. Who were the other four Celtic starters in the championship game?

**5.** The last championship in the Celtics' consecutive string was in 1966, with Boston beating Los Angeles. Who was with Russell that season?

**6.** The Lakers have been in more playoff games than any other team. They came close to winning many times after their move to Los Angeles, including 1962 when a last-second shot by Frank Selvy hung on the rim and fell away, allowing the Celtics to keep their streak alive. Who was in the Laker starting five that night along with Selvy?

**7.** In 1967, the Philadelphia 76ers broke the Celtic streak, first by defeating Boston in the Eastern playoffs, then by whipping San Francisco for the title. Name the Philadelphia starting five in the last game.

**8.** The only championship in the history of the Rochester-Cincinnati-Kansas City franchise came in 1951. Who were the mainstays of the Royal team that beat the Knicks?

**9.** The Lakers won their first NBA title in Los Angeles in

1972. What was the starting line-up for the championship game?

10. Syracuse's only championship came in 1955 with a 92-91 victory over Fort Wayne. Name the starting Nats.

# 71. Of Diamonds and Hardwood

*Many athletes have managed careers in both basketball and baseball. Identify the teams in those two sports that these athletes played with.*

1. Dick Groat
2. Gene Conley
3. Chuck Conners
4. Dave DeBusschere
5. Cotton Nash
6. Steve Hamilton
7. Ron Reed
8. Frankie Baumholtz
9. Hank Biasetti
10. Dick Ricketts
11. Howie Schultz

## 72. NIT Crown

*The National Invitation Tournament at Madison Square Garden is the oldest continuous post-season tourney for major college teams. Match the NIT champions on the left with their last opponent before claiming the crown. Championship game scores are included.*

1. West Virginia 47
2. St. Louis 65
3. Bradley 86
4. Temple 60
5. Seton Hall 58
6. Brigham Young 97
7. DePaul 71
8. Providence 81
9. Xavier (O.) 78
10. Temple 89
11. Dayton 73
12. CCNY 69
13. Louisville 93
14. Marquette 65
15. Kentucky 46
16. San Francisco 48
17. Southern Illinois 71
18. St. John's 55
19. North Carolina 84
20. Utah 49

a) St. John's 67
b) Kentucky 45
c) Loyola (Chicago) 47
d) Western Kentucky 45
e) Villanova 51
f) New York University 52
g) Georgia Tech 66
h) New Mexico 54
i) Marquette 56
j) Colorado 36
k) St. John's 46
l) Bowling Green 54
m) Rhode Island 45
n) NYU 84
o) Canisius 66
p) Bradley 61
q) Dusquesne 74
r) Dayton 80
s) Boston College 76
t) St. John's 53

## 73. NBA MVP

**1.** The NBA's Most Valuable Player receives the Podoloff Cup. Who was selected the league's first MVP in 1956?

**2.** Name the only two backcourt men to be named NBA MVP.

**3.** Name the player who was runner-up in the balloting four times, yet never won the award.

**4.** Which of these players was never selected MVP in an NBA All-Star Game:
- a) Dolph Schayes
- b) Bill Sharman
- c) Hal Greer
- d) Adrian Smith

**5.** In the 1962 All-Star Game, Wilt Chamberlain scored a record 42 points and hauled down 24 rebounds, yet was not the game's MVP. Who was?

**6.** Who is the only player to win Rookie of the Year honors and the Podoloff Cup in the same year?

**7.** The first East-West All-Star Game was played in Boston in 1951. What Celtic was the game's MVP?

**8.** *Sport* Magazine started selecting playoff MVPs in 1969. Who was the inaugural winner?

**9.** Which of these players was never named the league's MVP:
- a) Bill Russell
- b) Elgin Baylor
- c) Willis Reed
- d) Wilt Chamberlain

## 74. Amateur Ball

*Many a fine collegiate basketball player has continued his career with an amateur team in a league like the old National Industrial Basketball League, or in the national AAU championships. Match the cities on the left with the teams that represented them.*

1. Bartlesville
2. Peoria
3. Wichita
4. Lexington
5. Cleveland
6. Denver
7. Seattle
8. Akron
9. Oakland
10. New York
11. McPherston

a) Pipers
b) Buchan Bakers
c) Bittners
d) Globe Refiners
e) Phillips 66ers
f) Tuck Tapers
g) Caterpillars
h) Marathon Oils
i) D-C Truckers
j) Goodyears
k) Vickers

## 75. Cleaning the Boards

**1.** Who are the only two men, other than Bill Russell and Wilt Chamberlain, to grab 40 or more rebounds in an NBA game?

**2.** Rebounds were not a recorded statistic in the NBA until 1951. Who was the first rebound champion?

**3.** In 1955, for the first time, one team had two of the top five rebounders in the NBA. Name these two Knicks.

**4.** The most rebounds ever grabbed by a team in one season was 6,131 by the Boston Celtics during the 1960-61 season. Bill Russell was the team leader with 1,868, but who were the four other Celts who grabbed 400 or more?

**5.** Of the top ten all-time leading NBA rebounders, five played primarily at forward. Who were they?

**6.** Who set the ABA single-game rebound record with 40?

**7.** In the 1969-70 season, who set the ABA single-season rebound record with 1,637?

**8.** Who set the NBA All-Star Game rebound mark with 27 in the 1962 contest?

**9.** Who was the ABA's all-time career rebound leader?

# 76. Pro Firsts

**1.** Who were the first two blacks to coach in an NBA All-Star Game?

**2.** Who was the first, and only, man to play with a team in the NBA playoffs although he never appeared in a regular season game with that team?

**3.** Which team was the first champion of the ABA in its initial season of 1967-68?

**4.** Which was the first pro team to sign Ohio State All-American Jerry Lucas?

**5.** Back in 1946 when the NBA forerunner, the Basketball Association of America, held its first draft of college players, who was the first collegian selected?

**6.** It was the 1959-60 season before the NBA had a player who averaged 30 points a game for the season. Who were the first two men to surpass the 30-point barrier?

## 77. For the Birds

*Many memorable basketball moments have come from teams with nicknames of winged creatures. Match the teams on the left with the nicknames in the column on the right.*

1. Temple
2. Kansas
3. South Carolina
4. Iowa
5. Louisville
6. Bowling Green
7. Creighton
8. St. Joseph's
9. Long Island U.
10. Canisius
11. Boston College
12. Niagara
13. Oregon
14. Virginia Tech
15. St. Peter's

a) Cardinals
b) Blue Jays
c) Blackbirds
d) Eagles
e) Owls
f) Gamecocks
g) Webfoots
h) Peacocks
i) Jayhawks
j) Hawkeyes
k) Gobblers
l) Falcons
m) Hawks
n) Purple Eagles
o) Griffins

## 78. A Helping Hand

1. The first time he NBA's scoring leader and top assist maker were on the same team was 1952, when Philadelphia's Paul Arizin averaged 25.4 points a game. Who was Arizin's passing friend?

2. When San Francisco's Guy Rodgers tied an NBA record with 28 assists in a single game on March 14, 1963, who was the beneficiary of most of his feeds?

**3.** In the ABA, Billy Melchionni established a league record with 672 assists during the 1970-71 season. Who was his New York Net teammate who averaged 29.4 points a game, many of those points coming on passes from Melchionni?

**4.** Oscar Robertson holds the NBA All-Star Game record of 14 assists, set in the 1961 contest. What two St. Louis Hawks were on the receiving end of the Big O's passes?

**5.** Wilt Chamberlain led the NBA in assists during the 1967-68 season. What guard, who averaged a career-high 24.1 points that year, benefited the most?

**6.** In the ABA All-Star Game in 1974, Carolina's Mack Calvin accounted for a record 11 assists on passes to what two big men, one from the Nets, the other from the Colonels?

**7.** Jerry West was best known as a scorer, but he led the NBA in assists in 1972. Who was his 25.9-point scoring teammate, often on the receiving end?

**8.** When Oscar Robertson averaged an NBA record 11.5 assists a game during the 1964-65 season, who were his three Cincinnati teammates who were ranked with him among the league's top 25 scorers?

**9.** When Larry Brown played for Denver in the ABA he set a league mark with 23 assists in a game against Pittsburgh. What two teammates, each scoring 37 points, were on the receiving end?

**10.** When Wilt Chamberlain scored his record 100 points, the last two came off a feed from what Philadelphia teammate?

## 79. Once in the NBA

*Match the erstwhile NBA nicknames on the left with their cities.*

1. Packers
2. Steamrollers
3. Olympians
4. Nationals
5. Warriors
6. Zephyrs
7. Lakers
8. Zollner-Pistons
9. Stags
10. Bombers
11. Hawks
12. Redskins
13. Royals
14. Rebels

a) Milwaukee
b) Chicago
c) Fort Wayne
d) St. Louis
e) Providence
f) Sheboygan
g) Anderson
h) Cleveland
i) Indianapolis
j) Rochester
k) Philadelphia
l) Syracuse
m) Minneapolis
n) Chicago

# 80. Final Foe

*Match the NCAA champions on the left with the team they defeated in the championship game by the indicated scores.*

1. Texas Western 72
2. UCLA 80
3. Oregon 46
4. Ohio State 75
5. Wyoming 46
6. UCLA 79
7. Oklahoma A&M 49
8. California 71
9. Holy Cross 58
10. Indiana 69
11. North Carolina 54
12. UCLA 78
13. Indiana 60
14. UCLA 98
15. San Francisco 77
16. Kentucky 58
17. Wisconsin 39
18. UCLA 92
19. LaSalle 92
20. Oklahoma A&M 43
21. Kansas 80
22. San Francisco 83
23. Kentucky 84
24. Utah 42
25. Stanford 53
26. Kentucky 68

a) Dartmouth 40
b) Dartmouth 38
c) Bradley 76
d) Kentucky 65
e) North Carolina 40
f) Jacksonville 69
g) St. John's 63
h) Ohio State 33
i) Purdue 72
j) California 55
k) Iowa 71
l) Washington St. 34
m) Georgetown 43
n) Seattle 72
o) Dayton 64
p) Kansas State 58
q) New York University 45
r) Oklahoma 47
s) West Virginia 70
t) Baylor 42
u) Kansas 68
v) Kansas 53
w) Duke 83
x) North Carolina 55
y) Kansas 42
z) LaSalle 63

# 81. ABA Match-Ups

*Match the nicknames and teams for these former ABA franchises.*

1. Minnesota
2. Pittsburgh
3. Anaheim
4. Los Angeles
5. Dallas
6. Houston
7. Miami
8. Carolina
9. New Jersey
10. New Orleans
11. Washington
12. Memphis
13. San Diego
14. Oakland
15. Baltimore
16. Virginia

a) Stars
b) Floridians
c) Buccaneers
d) Oaks
e) Muskies
f) Conquistadors
g) Amigos
h) Chaparrals
i) Pros
j) Condors
k) Mavericks
l) Squires
m) Americans
n) Cougars
o) Capitals
p) Claws

## 82. All-Indian

Many collegiate teams use nicknames borrowed from the American Indians. Match the schools on the left, which have provided many memorable moments in basketball, with the nicknames on the right.

1. St. John's
2. Bradley
3. William & Mary
4. Oklahoma City
5. Miami (O.)
6. Seattle
7. North Dakota
8. Illinois
9. Marquette
10. San Diego State
11. Eastern Michigan
12. Central Michigan
13. Florida State

a) Redskins
b) Fighting Illini
c) Seminoles
d) Chieftains
e) Redmen
f) Chiefs
g) Braves
h) Fighting Sioux
i) Chippewas
j) Warriors
k) Indians
l) Hurons
m) Aztecs

## 83. Getting the Bounces

One thousand rebounds is a good number for any player to grab in one season, yet some teams have had two 1,000-rebound men in the same year. Match these NBA players with their teammates, each of whom grabbed 1,000 rebounds in the same season.

1. Bailey Howell
2. Dave Cowens
3. Wes Unseld
4. Nate Thurmond
5. Wilt Chamberlain
6. Walt Bellamy
7. Clyde Lee
8. Willis Reed

a) Happy Hairston
b) Paul Silas
c) Gus Johnson
d) Nate Thurmond
e) Walter Dukes
f) Walt Bellamy
g) Elvin Hayes
h) Jerry Lucas

## 84. College Scorers

**1.** Only three major college players have averaged 40 points a game during a basketball season. Name them.

**2.** What Villanova Wildcat was the nation's scoring leader in 1950, the year City College of New York won the NIT and NCAA championships?

**3.** Who was the Southwestern Louisiana player who poured in a record 1,445 field goals during his Ragin' Cajun career, which ended in 1973?

**4.** The end of the 1956-57 season saw scorers like Wilt Chamberlain of Kansas and Elgin Baylor of Seattle finish behind what South Carolina Gamecock for scoring honors?

**5.** What Paladin tossed in a record 355 free throws for Furman during the 1953-54 season?

**6.** Ohio State and Cincinnati battled for the NCAA crown for the second year in a row in 1962, but who was the Utah center who walked off with national scoring honors?

**7.** The highest-scoring player in Ivy League history poured in 2,503 points and averaged 30.2 points per game at Princeton. Name him.

**8.** The closest battle for the NCAA scoring championship came during the 1962-63 season when what Seton Hall Pirate bested what New York U. Violet by .2 of a point?

**9.** The single-season scoring record for a player from the Mid-American conference is 36.7 points per game, set by what Bowling Green Falcon in 1964?

**10.** Who is the Wake Forest deadeye who tossed in a record 905 free throws during his four varsity years, 1952-55?

## 85. Old Homes

Match the arenas on the left with the NBA teams that once called them home.

1. Kiel Auditorium
2. Cow Palace
3. Sports Arena
4. Hofheinz Pavilion
5. Cole Field House

a) Rockets
b) Bullets
c) Hawks
d) Lakers
e) Warriors

## 86. One of a Kind

Despite the fact that hundreds of players have come and gone in the NBA, there have been some men who were the only ones to have a first name like their own. Supply the last names for:

1. Med
2. Hub
3. Ossie
4. Shellie
5. Si
6. Donnis
7. Zelmo
8. Ephraim
9. Togo
10. Toby
11. Slater
12. Dorrie
13. Marko

79

## 87. AAU All-Stars

**1.** The AAU national basketball champions in 1966 were the Ford Mustangs, and the tourney MVP was a U. of Michigan player who later turned pro with the New York Knicks. Name him.

**2.** The 1941 AAU tourney went to 20th-Century Fox, but the top player that season was a Stanford athlete playing for the San Francisco Olympic Club. Who was he?

**3.** A noted collegiate and Olympic basketball coach was on the 1931 AAU titlists sponsored by Henry Clothiers of Wichita, Kansas. Name this player who later coached at Oklahoma A&M.

**4.** A former Marquette all-star led the Phillips 66ers to the AAU crown in 1963, earning MVP honors for himself. Later he enjoyed a 12-year NBA career. Name him.

**5.** A coach in the ABA and an assistant coach in the NBA, who was the St. Mary's player who was tourney MVP with the San Francisco Olympic Club team in 1957?

**6.** A winning head coach in the ABA, who was the one-time North Carolina player who was named MVP in the 1964 tournament with the Akron Goodyears?

**7.** Who was the bruising rebounder who was an AAU All-American and mainstay of the champion 20th-Century Fox team of the early 1940s?

**8.** Two of the first blacks to play in the NBA were AAU All-Americans in 1950 with the Oakland Blue 'N Gold squad. Name these former UCLA players.

**9.** One of the stars of the U.S. Olympic team in 1948 and 1952, who was the former Oklahoma A&M player who led the Phillips 66ers to the AAU championship in 1948 and 1950?

**10.** What one-time St. Louis U. star played with the Wichita Vickers in 1959, leading them to the AAU title and capturing MVP honors for himself?

## 88. Fast Break

*Match these eight cities which were represented in the American Basketball League's initial season of 1961-62, with their team's nicknames.*

1. Cleveland           a) Tapers
2. Pittsburgh          b) Jets
3. Chicago             c) Chiefs
4. Washington          d) Pipers
5. Kansas City         e) Majors
6. Los Angeles         f) Saints
7. San Francisco       g) Rens
8. Hawaii              h) Steers

## 89. ABL Legacy

*The American Basketball League lived briefly in the early 1960s, and one of its few legacies was the 3-point field goal which survived in the American Basketball Association of a few years later.*

1. Washington was an original ABL city, but where did the franchise move after its first season?

2. What noted basketball personality was the first commissioner of the ABL?

3. The first black head coach of a major professional basketball team was in the ABL. Who was he, and what team did he coach?

4. What player, who later starred in both the ABA and NBA, was the ABL's leading scorer with a 27.5-point average?

5. Which team was the only champion the league ever had?

6. Which of these players were ABL stars:
    a) Al Attles
    b) Dick Barnett
    c) Bill Bridges
    d) Ken Sears
    e) Bob Leonard
    f) Al Bianchi
    g) Mike Farmer
    h) Hub Reed

# SPORTS & MOVIES

## 90. Featured Performer

*Identify the sports personalities who were the central figures in these films.*

1. *Babe*
2. *Follow the Sun*
3. *It's Great to Be Alive*
4. *Maurice*
5. *Go, Man, Go*
6. *Crazylegs*
7. *Run to Daylight*


## 91. Stars and the Silver Screen

*Match these sports stars and the films they played in.*

| | | | |
|---|---|---|---|
| 1. | Joe Namath | a) | *100 Rifles* |
| 2. | Hank Luisetti | b) | *The 10th Cavalry* |
| 3. | Alex Karras | c) | *Shanghai Gesture* |
| 4. | Dan Pastorini | d) | *Sweetheart of Sigma Chi* |
| 5. | Bernie Casey | e) | *The Undefeated* |
| 6. | Jack Snow | f) | *Combat Correspondent* |
| 7. | Milt Plum | g) | *Andy Hardy Steps Out* |
| 8. | Jim Brown | h) | *The Paper Lion* |
| 9. | Dick Bass | i) | *Blazing Saddles* |
| 10. | Johnny Weissmuller | j) | *Guns of the Magnificent Seven* |
| 11. | Rafer Johnson | k) | *Campus Confessions* |
| 12. | Mike Mazurki | l) | *Weed* |
| 13. | Esther Williams | m) | *Marooned* |
| 14. | Roman Gabriel | n) | *The Grasshopper* |
| 15. | Buster Crabbe | o) | *The Games* |
| 16. | Otis Taylor | p) | *C.C. & Company* |

## 92. Play Acting

*Name the actors who portrayed the following athletes on the screen:*

1. Ben Hogan in *Follow the Sun*
2. Brian Piccolo in *Brian's Song*
3. Gale Sayers in *Brian's Song*
4. Jim Corbett in *Gentleman Jim*
5. Jack Johnson in *The Great White Hope*
6. George Zaharias in *Babe*
7. Babe Didrikson in *Babe*
8. Babe Ruth in *The Babe Ruth Story*
9. Joe Louis in *The Joe Louis Story*
10. John L. Sullivan in *The Great John L*
11. Knute Rockne in *Knute Rockne—All-American*
12. Roy Campanella in *It's Great to Be Alive*

## 93. Made in Heaven

*Match the sports heroes on the right with the movie stars they married.*

1. Marilyn Monroe
2. Jane Russell
3. Barbara Darrow
4. Terry Moore
5. Laraine Day
6. Estelle Taylor
7. Elyse Knox
8. Diana Barrymore

a) Tom Harmon
b) Leo Durocher
c) John Lawson
d) Joe DiMaggio
e) Pancho Gonzalez
f) Bob Waterfield
g) Glenn Davis
h) Jack Dempsey

## 94. Cinema Subject

*Make the connection between the film on the left and the sport which is integral to the movie's theme, on the right.*

1. *The Hustler*
2. *The Racers*
3. *Bang the Drum Slowly*
4. *Body and Soul*
5. *Blood and Sand*
6. *Pylon*
7. *Junior Bonner*
8. *Kansas City Bomber*
9. *The Duke of West Point*
10. *Pat and Mike*
11. *Drive, He Said*
12. *National Velvet*
13. *That's My Boy*
14. *Saturday Night, Sunday Morning*

a) Roller Derby
b) Tennis
c) Horse racing
d) Pocket billiards
e) Hockey
f) Basketball
g) Auto Racing
h) Boxing
i) Rugby
j) Football
k) Bullfighting
l) Airplane racing
m) Rodeo
n) Baseball

# 95. Sports in the Background

*Match these movie stars with their sport and college.*

1. Burt Reynolds
2. Kirk Douglas
3. Woody Strode
4. Robert Ryan
5. James Garner

6. Mike Conners
7. Dick Gregory

8. Burt Lancaster
9. Vince Edwards
10. Jack Palance
11. John Wayne
12. Johnny Mack Brown

13. Bill Cosby
14. Chuck Connors

a) Football, Oklahoma
b) Track, Southern Illinois
c) Swimming, Ohio State
d) Football, Florida State
e) Football, Southern California
f) Wrestling, St. Lawrence
g) Baseball & Basketball, Seton Hall
h) Football, UCLA
i) Basketball, UCLA
j) Football, Temple
k) Boxing, Dartmouth
l) Basketball, New York University
m) Football, North Carolina
n) Football, Alabama

# BOXING

## 96. Dethroned

*The fighters on the left won their world championships by dethroning which weight-class champions?*

1. Joe Louis
2. Billy Conn
3. Red Cochrane
4. John Henry Lewis
5. Henry Armstrong
6. Henry Armstrong
7. Henry Armstrong
8. Andre Routis
9. Kid Chocolate

10. Jersey Joe Walcott
11. Jack Dempsey
12. Maxie Rosenbloom

a) Fritzie Zivic (welter)
b) Barney Ross (welter)
c) Benny Bass (feather)
d) Jess Willard (heavy)
e) Tony Canzoneri (feather)
f) Ezzard Charles (heavy)
g) James Braddock (heavy)
h) Malio Bettina (light heavy)
i) Jimmy Slattery (light heavy)
j) Lou Ambers (light)
k) Bob Olin (light heavy)
l) Petey Sarron (feather)


## 97. Champs from Abroad

*Only five non-Americans have held the heavyweight boxing championship of the world. Which of these are they?*

a) Bob Fitzsimmons
b) Paulino Uzcudun
c) Georges Carpentier
d) Tommy Burns
e) Tony Galento
f) Max Schmeling
g) Arturo Godoy
h) Primo Carnera
i) Tom Heeney
j) Ingemar Johansson

# 98. It's All History

**1.** Joey Giardello made one successful defense of his middleweight crown. Whom did he defeat?

**2.** Which champion (any weight) had the most knockouts against major opposition?

**3.** Who was the boxer who was a church deacon and recited a psalm before each fight?

**4.** What boxer won a world championship more often than any other fighter, five times?

**5.** The oldest man to hold a world title was what American who gained the lightheavyweight championship in June, 1961, at age 44?

**6.** The shortest reign of any heavyweight champion was less than a year, June 29, 1933 to June 14, 1934. Who was he?

**7.** The Broadway play and Hollywood movie "The Great White Hope" told of the exploits of heavyweight champion Jack Johnson. He lost the title to whom in a 26th-round knockout in Havana on April 5, 1915?

**8.** When Muhammad Ali, then Cassius Clay, was stripped of his heavyweight championship on March 22, 1967, he was undefeated in how many fights?

**9.** The largest in-person attendance at a fight was 135,132 in Milwaukee's lakefront Juneau Park on August 18, 1941. Whom did they come to see?

**10.** Who was the Penn State all-star athlete and boxer who beat Max Schmeling in 1934, only to lose to the German a year later in a fight that ended his career.

**11.** One of the shortest, if not *the* shortest, championship reigns was that of a British middleweight who held the title from July 10 to September 15, 1951. Name him.

## 99. Monikers

*Hook up the nicknames on the left with the fighters who carried them.*

1. Livermore Larruper
2. Brockton Blockbuster
3. Boston Gob
4. Boston Strongboy
5. Philadelphia Dance Master
6. Basque Woodchopper
7. Tall Tower of Gorgonzola
8. Hard Rock Down Under
9. Cinderella Man
10. Aberdeen Assassin
11. Toy Bulldog
12. Hurricane

a) Leo Lomski
b) Tom Heeney
c) Paulino Uzcudun
d) Max Baer
e) Jack Sharkey
f) Mickey Walker
g) Rocky Marciano
h) John L. Sullivan
i) Tommy Loughran
j) Tommy Jackson
k) Primo Carnera
l) James J. Braddock

## 100. In the Same Boat

*What thing do these former world champions all have in common?*

Jake LaMotta
Randy Turpin
Carl "Bobo" Olson
Gene Fullmer
Carmen Basilio

## 101. Identity Change

*Boxers often change their name before stepping into the ring. Match the ring personalities on the left with their "other" names.*

1. Tommy Burns
2. Muhammad Ali
3. Young Corbett
4. Jack Sharkey
5. Pancho Villa
6. Kid McCoy
7. Joe Louis
8. Jersey Joe Walcott
9. Kid Gavilan
10. Sugar Ray Robinson

a) Joseph Paul Kukauskas
b) Norman Selby
c) Arnold Cream
d) Walker Smith
e) Noah Brusso
f) Gerardo Gonzales
g) Cassius Clay
h) Francisco Guilledo
i) William Rothwell
j) Joseph Barrow

# TENNIS

## 102. Racket Country

*Match these tennis stars with their homelands.*

1. Bjorn Borg
2. Ilie Nastase
3. Jan Kodes
4. Vijay Amritraj
5. Tom Okker
6. Manuel Orantes
7. Nikki Pilic
8. Raul Ramirez
9. Jaime Fillol
10. Patrice Dominguez
11. Onny Parun
12. Alex Metreveli
13. Karl Meiler
14. Guillermo Vilas
15. Adriano Panatta
16. Cliff Drysdale
17. John Alexander
18. Ivan Molina
19. Wojtek Fibak
20. Vitas Gerulaitis
21. Andy Pattison
22. Roger Taylor

a) Colombia
b) Yugoslavia
c) France
d) Germany
e) Italy
f) South Africa
g) Poland
h) Rhodesia
i) Great Britain
j) Sweden
k) Czechoslovakia
l) Netherlands
m) Mexico
n) New Zealand
o) United States
p) Romania
q) Spain
r) India
s) Chile
t) Soviet Union
u) Argentina
v) Australia

## 103. Campus Netmen

*Match the schools where these future pro tennis stars won NCAA titles, either as singles or doubles players.*

1. Pancho Segura
2. Charles Pasarell
3. Barry MacKay
4. Tony Trabert
5. Rafael Osuna
6. Whitney Reed
7. Ron Holmberg

a) Cincinnati
b) San Jose State
c) Miami (Fla.)
d) Southern California
e) Tulane
f) Michigan
g) UCLA

## 104. Women Aces

*Match up these international tennis stars with the country they represent.*

1. Isabel Fernandez
2. Olga Morozova
3. Karen Krantzcke
4. Marie Neumannova
5. Virginia Wade
6. Françoise Durr
7. Ilana Kloss
8. Rosie Casals
9. Heide Orth

a) Australia
b) France
c) United States
d) Colombia
e) South Africa
f) Soviet Union
g) West Germany
h) Czechoslovakia
i) Great Britain

# OLYMPICS

# 105. Water Kings

**1.** Who was the American who won four swimming gold medals at Tokyo in 1964?

**2.** What New York Athletic Club swimmer used the newfangled "crawl" stroke to dominate the swimming events at the 1904 Olympics in St. Louis?

**3.** The U.S. men were anything but dominant in the 1950s, winning only three individual gold medals at Helsinki in 1952. Name that year's 1500-meter freestyle, 100-meter freestyle, and 100-meter backstroke champions from the U.S.

**4.** At Melbourne in 1956, American men won only one gold medal, in the 200-meter butterfly. Name the man who won it.

**5.** Name the Hawaiian with the flutter kick who won the gold medal for the U.S. in the 100-meter freestyle at Stockholm in 1912.

**6.** The 4x100-meter medley relay was introduced to Olympic competition at Rome in 1960, and the U.S. won it and every medal in this event since then. Name the quartet who captured the inaugural contest.

**7.** Who was the long-distance swimming star for the U.S. in the 1920 Games at Antwerp, winning the 400- and 1500-meter freestyles?

**8.** Who was the East German who was the only non-American to win two gold medals at Mexico City in 1968?

**9.** Johnny Weissmuller won three gold medals at Paris in 1924, including the 4x200-meter freestyle relay. Who were his teammates on the relay?

**10.** Name the seven events in which Mark Spitz won his gold medals at Munich in 1972.

**11.** Buster Crabbe went from Olympic glory to Hollywood movie stardom as Tarzan. What swimming event did he win at Los Angeles in 1932?

**12.** Which was the only swimming event the U.S. men failed to win at Montreal in 1976, and who won it?

# 106. Women Olympians

*For what countries did these female Olympians win their gold medals?*

1. Skier Christel Cranz
2. Swimmer Dawn Fraser
3. Figure skater Barbara Ann Scott
4. Fencer Helene Mayer
5. Sprinter Fanny Blankers-Koen
6. Figure skater Sonja Henie
7. Discus thrower Olga Fikotova
8. Sprinter Stella Walsh
9. Skier Nancy Greene
10. Shotputter/discus thrower Tamara Press

# 107. Mat Masters

**1.** Russian Levan Tediashvili won the middleweight freestyle wrestling gold medal at Munich, then moved up to the light heavyweight class at Montreal. What two American brothers did he beat to win the respective medals?

**2.** Name the U.S. light heavyweight who won more than 300 matches during his career, including the Olympic championship at London in 1948.

**3.** American wrestlers made their best showing in 28 years in the 1960 games at Rome. Name the trio who won gold medals in the bantamweight, lightweight, and welterweight divisions.

**4.** Three Americans also won gold medals at Munich in 1972. Name the lightweight, welterweight, and light heavyweight champions of that year.

**5.** Who was the 400-pounder from Iowa State who earned a bronze medal for the U.S. in 1972.

**6.** Name the lone American wrestler to win a gold medal in 1976 at Montreal.

## 108. Fisticuffs

**1.** The U.S. boxing team took seven gold medals in the St. Louis Olympics of 1904, but didn't have another showing like that until 1952 in Helsinki, where they won five golds. Name the quintet of champions.

**2.** Two U.S. boxers who won gold medals at Antwerp went on to gain more fame. The flyweight winner became a professional fight champion, while the light heavyweight medalist won a gold medal as a bobsledder in 1932, thus becoming the only man to win both summer and winter gold medals. Name this pair.

**3.** A welterweight from Tacoma, Washington, was the only American to win a gold medal for boxing in Munich in 1972. Who is he?

**4.** Who was the Italian welterweight who won a gold medal in Rome in 1960 before turning professional and becoming a champion of the world?

**5.** Two future professional titleholders won gold medals for the U.S. in Paris in 1924. Name the flyweight and featherweight Olympic champs of that year.

**6.** Who is the Hungarian fighter who is the only man to win three gold medals in Olympic boxing, in 1948, 1952, and 1956?

**7.** Two Americans won gold medals at Los Angeles in 1932, and it would be 20 years before Americans won another. Name the welterweight and middleweight titlists of 1932.

**8.** Name the 1956 heavyweight gold medal winner from the U.S. whose first professional fight was for the heavyweight championship.

**9.** An Argentinian runner-up in the flyweight division in Amsterdam in 1928 later turned pro and won the world title. Name him.

**10.** Another Argentinian flyweight champion—both Olympic and professional—made his mark in the London games of 1948 when he jumped into the swimming pool after winning the gold medal. Who was he?

**11.** When Muhammad Ali—then Cassius Marcellus Clay—won a gold medal in 1960, what was his weight class?

## 109. Court Play

**1.** The U.S. won its first Olympic basketball championship at Berlin in 1936 in a title game played outdoors in a driving rainstorm. The Americans won, 19-8. Who lost?

**2.** Who was the Russian who scored the basket that beat the U.S. in the disputed championship game in Munich in 1972?

**3.** Whose free throws had apparently won the game for the Americans before that final Russian shot in 1972?

**4.** The U.S. basketball team of 1960 was called the best, ever. How many of the 12 squad members can you name?

**5.** Who was the 7-foot redhead who led Americans to victory in 1948 and 1952?

**6.** Bill Russell was the center on the U.S. five in Melbourne in 1956. Who were the other big guns on that team?

**7.** The 1968 U.S. basketball squad was a gold medal winner despite the absence of such stars as Lew Alcindor, Elvin Hayes, and Wes Unseld. Who were the dominating big man and backcourt pair that controlled American fortunes in Mexico City?

**8.** Ten Americans shared the playing time at Tokyo in 1964 as the U.S. won its sixth straight basketball gold medal. Name the ten.

# 110. Running for Gold

*Match the trackmen in the left-hand column with the events in which they won Olympic gold medals.*

1. Harrison Dillard
2. Horace Ashenfelter
3. Glenn Davis
4. Otis Davis
5. Billy Mills
6. Henry Carr
7. Tom Courtney
8. Bob Schul
9. Bill Porter
10. Frank Shorter

a) 10,000 meters
b) 800 meters
c) 5,000 meters
d) Marathon
e) Steeplechase
f) 110-meter hurdles
g) 400-meter hurdles
h) 100 meters
i) 400 meters
j) 200 meters

## 111. Manning the Lifts

**1.** The most memorable weightlifter of the 1956 games in Melbourne was what mammoth Georgia boy who won the heavyweight gold medal for the U.S.?

**2.** Who was the diminutive bantamweight who set a world record in winning the gold medal for America at London in 1948?

**3.** Another bantamweight was the only U.S. weightlifter to get a gold medal in Rome in 1960 as he successfully defended his Olympic championship. Name him.

**4.** One of America's best weightlifters earned a silver medal in 1948, a gold in 1952, a bronze in 1960, and a bronze in 1964. Who is he?

**5.** Who is the U.S. lifter who established a world record in Helsinki in 1952 and came back four years later to win the gold in a heavier class?

## 112. A Jump in the Water

*Men's Division*

**1.** Who was the American diver who won both the springboard and platform gold medals in the 1924 Olympics in Paris?

**2.** Another American duplicated the Olympic double at Amsterdam in 1928. Name him.

**3.** What Army officer and physician won gold medals for platform diving at both London and Helsinki?

**4.** The only other American to win Olympic gold medals in successive games was what platform diver in 1960 and 1964?

**5.** Who is the Italian diver who won an unprecedented third gold medal when he took the platform competition at Montreal in 1976?

*Women's Division*

**6.** What U.S. woman is the only diver—male or female—to win both diving events in two successive Olympic Games?

**7.** In 1920, a 13-year-old from the U.S. won the springboard diving gold medal, and her 14-year-old teammate won the silver. Name them.

**8.** Who was the U.S. diver who won both the platform and springboard competitions at the 1948 Olympics in London?

**9.** The first time an American didn't win one of the two Olympic diving events was in Rome in 1960 when what 17-year-old German won both gold medals?

**10.** The youngest U.S. gold medal winner ever was what springboard diver who topped the competition at Berlin in 1936?

# 113. On the Track

**1.** The only American ever to win the Olympic 3,000-meter steeplechase was an FBI man who ran to glory at Helsinki in 1952. Name him.

**2.** The American sprinters were shut out of the individual medals at Munich in 1972 because of a scheduling mixup, but they came back to win the 4x100-meter relay. Name the winning quartet.

**3.** Who were the two runners, the first and third finishers, in the 200 meters who got in trouble for raising "black power" salutes during the medal ceremonies in Mexico City in 1968?

**4.** Jesse Owens led America's "black auxiliaries" at Berlin in 1936, but he didn't do the job alone. Which of his two fellow auxiliaries won the 400- and 800-meter events?

**5.** The finish of the 800 meters in Helsinki was the same as it had been in London in 1948, with an American winning and a Jamaican capturing the silver medal. Name the pair.

**6.** The 1960 Games in Rome were among the least productive in terms of gold medals for the U.S., as only two American runners won individual gold medals, in the 400 meters and 400-meter hurdles. Name the winners.

**7.** At Tokyo in 1964, the U.S. won every running event from the 100 up to the 10,000 meters, except for the 800 and 1,500. One man captured both those competitions. Name him.

**8.** The last time an American won both sprints was at Melbourne in 1956. Who turned the trick?

**9.** The finish of the 5,000-meter run in Los Angeles in 1932 was controversial, as most witnesses thought Finland's gold medal winner Lauri Lehtinen interfered with what U.S. runner?

**10.** Who was the golf-capped victor in the 800 meters at Munich in 1972?

## 114. A Bevy of Babes

**1.** What American woman is the only sprinter—male or female—to win the 100-meter gold medal in two different Olympic Games?

**2.** The last time an American woman won an Olympic field event was in 1956 at Melbourne. Who was that high jump gold medalist that year?

**3.** Babe Didrikson of the U.S. won two of the three events she entered in Los Angeles in 1932, losing only the high jump, where she was runner-up. What other American won the event?

**4.** Who was the Dutch woman known as Fabulous Fanny who won four gold medals at London in 1948?

**5.** What 100-meter champion was America's only female track and field champion at Berlin in 1936?

**6.** Two women named Kathy, one in the 400 meters the other in the javelin, were the only individual medal winners for the U.S. at Munich in 1972. Name these bronze medal winners.

**7.** The last time an American relay team won a gold medal was 1968 in the 4x100-meter event. Name the triumphant foursome.

**8.** Who was the 1956 women's discus champion from Czechoslovakia, who later emmigrated to the U.S. and became a citizen?

**9.** Rome, 1960, marked the first time an American woman won three gold medals in track and field in one Olympics. Name her.

**10.** The only track and field gold medal for U.S. women at Helsinki in 1952 was in the 4x100-meter relay. Who earned it?

# 115. Gold Fields

**1.** Who introduced the "flop" to the world by winning the Olympic high jump at Mexico City in 1968?

**2.** The first black man to win an Olympic gold medal for the U.S. was what long jumper at Paris in 1924?

**3.** Jesse Owens was not the first American black champion snubbed by Adolph Hitler at the 1936 Games. Name the high jump champion who also was snubbed.

**4.** The first 60-foot plus shot put in Olympic history came in 1956 by what American gold medalist?

**5.** The world record in the long jump was broken by nearly two feet in 1968 by what U.S. leaper?

**6.** Mexico City also marked the fourth consecutive gold medal performance by what American discus thrower?

**7.** What U.S. pole vaulter is the only athlete to win the event more than once, when he captured gold in 1952 and 1956?

**8.** Who was the long jump champion at Berlin in 1936 whose record stood until the 1960 Games?

**9.** The only gold medal in a field event for U.S. men in 1972 came in the long jump. Who won it?

**10.** The last American sweep in the shot put came at Helsinki in 1952. Name the gold, silver, and bronze medalists of that year.

# 116. Water Queens

**1.** Who was the leader of the U.S. "water babies" at the 1960 Olympic Games in Rome?

**2.** The first full-scale swimming program for women was held at the Antwerp Games in 1920. Who was the American woman who won three gold medals that year?

**3.** She "trained on champagne" and was booted off the U.S. squad en route to Berlin in 1936, despite being the defending 100-meter backstroke champion. Name her.

**4.** Who was the 15-year-old whose victories in the 200-, 400-, and 800-meter freestyle events at Mexico City earned her the Sullivan Award as America's top amateur athlete of 1968?

**5.** What stately beauty, holder of 15 world records, won three gold medals for the U.S. at Los Angeles in 1932?

**6.** The U.S. women won only a single gold medal in 1948. Name the 400-meter freestyle champion of those Games.

**7.** The victorious United States 4x100-meter freestyle relay team at Paris in 1924 included Ethel Lackie, Mariechen Wehselau, and Euphrasia Donelly. What future long-distance star was the fourth member of the team?

**8.** Who was the Australian woman who won three consecutive 100-meter freestyle competitions between 1956 and 1964?

**9.** Tokyo, in 1964, was a good Olympics for American females as they won five gold medals. The top gold-getter was what 100-meter butterfly champion, who also swam on two winning relay teams?

**10.** The 1950s were a rough time for American women swimmers, as they won only one gold medal. That came in the 100-meter butterfly at Melbourne in 1956. Who won it?

**11.** What Australian teen-ager was the only non-American to win more than one gold medal at Munich in 1972?

## 117. Flags of All Nations

*The names of these gold medalists may be familiar, but can you identify the country for which they competed?*

1. Skier Toni Sailer
2. Long distance runner Emil Zatopek
3. Hurdler John Akii-Bua
4. Boxer Horace "Lefty" Gwynne
5. Swimmer Jon Konrads
6. Diver Klaus DiBiasi
7. Distance runner Paavo Nurmi
8. Middle distance runner Herb McKenley
9. Boxer Pascual Perez
10. Marathon runner Abebe Bikila
11. Yachtsman Prince Constantine

# HOCKEY

## 118. Iron Men

**1.** Who holds the record for having played in 82 games during the 1971-72 NHL season, when each team played only 78 games?

**2.** When Garry Unger set an NHL record by playing in his 631st straight game in 1976, whose record of 630 consecutive games played did he break?

**3.** Who played goal every minute of 502 games in a row between October, 1955 and November, 1962?

**4.** Who appeared in goal in 971 games, more than any other NHL goalie?

**5.** Gordie Howe holds the career record with 1,687 games played between 1946 and 1971. Who is the only other player to have appeared in more than 1,500 regular-season NHL games?

## 119. Adding Up

**1.** Name the six teams which were added for the 1967-68 NHL season, which doubled the size of the league.

**2.** Who was the first player taken in the expansion draft?

**3.** All six expansion teams were in the same division in their first season. Who finished on top?

**4.** Which expansion club was the first to play in a Stanley Cup final series.

**5.** Which expansion team was the first to win the Stanley Cup?

**6.** What two teams were added to the league in 1970?

**7.** In 1969, the first player from an expansion team won the Calder Cup as Rookie of the Year. Name him.

**8.** What two teams were added in 1972?

**9.** What Philadelphia Flyer was the first expansion team player to win the Hart Trophy as league MVP?

**10.** What two teams were added in 1974?

**11.** The 1968 season saw an expansion team player win the Conn Smythe Trophy as MVP in the playoffs. Name the goalie who was honored.

**12.** It wasn't until the 1973-74 season that an expansion team player, other than a goalie, was named to the first All-Star team. Who was the left-winger who made it?

# 120. Penalty Shot

**1.** The date was April 9, 1968 and the teams were Minnesota and Los Angeles when the only successful penalty shot in NHL playoff history was scored. Who were the King goalie and North Star shooter involved.

**2.** What future NHL coach scored the first-ever goal on a penalty shot when, playing for the St. Louis Maroons, he blasted one past Montreal goalie Alex Connell on November 13, 1934?

**3.** The first penalty shot ever taken in the NHL was by Armand Mondeau of Montreal on November 10, 1934. What all-time great goalie was in the Maple Leaf net to stop the shot?

**4.** The Washington Capitals may not have had the best team in the league during their first season, yet they accomplished something no other team did during the 1974-75 season by twice scoring goals on penalty shots. Name the Caps who did it.

## 121. NHL Trophy

**1.** The Art Ross Trophy goes to the top scorer each season. The last time a New York Ranger won it was 1942. Name him.

**2.** The Lady Byng Trophy is awarded for gentlemanly sportsmanship. The first player from an expansion club to win it was what St. Louis Blue in 1970?

**3.** Two men have won the Art Ross Trophy for scoring honors four years in a row. Name them.

**4.** The Most Valuable Player Award, the Hart Trophy, has been won by a Toronto Maple Leaf player only twice. Name the 1944 and 1955 recipients.

**5.** In 1967 and 1968 the same man won the Art Ross Trophy, Hart Trophy, and Lady Byng Trophy both seasons. Name him.

**6.** Who is the only Montreal Canadien ever to win the Lady Byng Trophy?

**7.** The Norris Trophy, first given in 1954, is awarded to the league's top defensemen. In its first 20 years, only seven different men won it. Name them.

**8.** Frankie Brimsek was the first Boston Bruin to win the Calder Trophy as Rookie of the Year, in 1939. Since then, four other Bruins have been so honored. Name them.

**9.** Who were the two St. Louis Blues who shared the Vezina Trophy as the league's top goaltenders for the 1968-69 season?

**10.** The first Connie Smythe Trophy—for Most Valuable Player in the Stanley Cup playoffs—was awarded to what Montreal Canadien in 1965?

**11.** In the 1950s, three different Canadiens won the NHL scoring championship and the Art Ross Trophy with it. Name them.

**12.** The Bill Masterson Trophy is given for perseverance and dedication. Name the Montreal Canadien who was the first recipient in 1968.

**13.** Since World War II, the Chicago Black Hawks have had three rookies who received the Calder Trophy. Name the 1955, 1960, and 1970 winners.

**14.** Only one man has won both the Hart and Smythe trophies as regular-season and playoff MVP in the same year. Who turned the trick in 1970 and again in 1972?

**15.** The last time a Toronto Maple Leaf led the NHL in scoring and gained the Art Ross Trophy was 1938. Who was it?

# 122. It's Still Detroit

*The Detroit National Hockey League club has had several nicknames. Which of these is not one of them?*

  a) Falcons
  b) Winged Wheels
  c) Cougars
  d) Red Wings

## 123. Brothers

*Provide the family name for these sets of NHL brothers.*

1. Max, Doug, and Red.
2. Marcel, Jean, and Claude.
3. Barclay, Bob, and Bill.
4. George, Frank, Billy, and Bob.
5. Brian, Barry, and Ray.
6. Jack, Jim, and Fred.
7. Roy, Charlie, and Lionel.

## 124. By the Numbers

1. The Boston Bruins retired uniform No. 2 in honor of what defenseman who played for them between 1926 and 1940?

2. The Detroit Red Wings retired the uniform numbers of both Gordie Howe and Alex Delvecchio. What were they?

3. Who wore No. 11 so memorably for the Vancouver Canucks that the team retired it?

4. The Montreal Canadiens retired numbers 4, 7, and 9. Who wore them?

5. The highest number retired by an NHL team is 19. Who wore it for the Minnesota North Stars?

6. What defensemen wore No. 2 before the Buffalo Sabres retired it in his honor?

## 125. Nicknames on Ice

*Supply the nicknames for these NHL greats.*

1. Aubrey _____ Clapper
2. Ralph _____ Weiland
3. Ivan _____ Johnson
4. Hector _____ Blake
5. Reginald _____ Smith
6. Emile _____ Bouchard
7. Cecil _____ Thompson
8. Edouard _____ Lalonde
9. Ernest _____ Johnson
10. Duncan _____ Mackay
11. John _____ Stewart
12. David _____ Schriner
13. Cecil _____ Dye
14. Harold _____ Simpson
15. Clarence _____ Day
16. George _____ Boucher
17. Russell _____ Stanley
18. Didier _____ Pitre
19. Allan _____ Davidson
20. Albert _____ Siebert
21. Walter _____ Broda
22. Wilfred _____ Green
23. Harry _____ Holmes
24. Harvey _____ Jackson
25. Francis Michael _____ Clancy

## 126. Stanley Cup

*Of the many hockey teams that have played in the Stanley Cup finals, a number no longer exist. Among these are the teams on the left. Match them with their nicknames.*

1. Montreal
2. Ottawa
3. Victoria
4. Toronto
5. Seattle
6. New York
7. Quebec
8. Vancouver
9. Kenora
10. Brandon

a) Cougars
b) Metropolitans
c) Bulldogs
d) Thistles
e) Maroons
f) St. Patricks
g) Wheat Kings
h) Senators
i) Americans
j) Millionaires

# GOLF

## 127. Who Am I?

*Identify these linksmen of note by the clues they might themselves give.*

**1.** I joined the pro tour in 1954, the year after I won the U.S. Amateur title. In 1961, I was U.S. Open champion and I've been on a dozen different Ryder Cup teams. In the course of winning more than 25 titles in 20 years on the PGA tour, I've been called "the machine."

**2.** I won the U.S. Open championship in 1969 and believe it or not that is my only tournament victory. I was born in Oklahoma and went to OU in Norman, but I didn't become a pro golfer until 1967, when I was 34 years old.

**3.** Gainesville is big in my life, since I was born in Gainesville, Ga., and went to college in Gainesville, Fla., at the University of Florida. I was runner-up in the U.S. Amateur tournament in 1958, and after I turned pro in 1961, I won the Canadian Open in 1969, beating Sam Snead in an 18-hole playoff, and was a member of the Ryder Cup teams in 1969 and 1973.

**4.** I'm an Easterner, born in Connecticut and still living in the New York metropolitan area. I won my first tournament in 1952, it was the Jacksonville Open, two years after joining the tour. I've won money every year since then (until 1976). My best year was 1957 when I took the Masters, Los Angeles Open, and Western Open.

**5.** My biggest earnings year was 1968 when I won $150,972 by taking the Pensacola and New Orleans tournaments as well as the National Team title with Bobby Nichols as a partner. I joined the tour in 1964 and five years later I won the Masters, beating Billy Casper, George Knudson, and Tom Weiskopf by a stroke.

**6.** I was Golfer of the Year for 1958, the year I won the PGA championship as well as the Utah Open. I started on the tour in 1952 after getting out of Ohio U. in my hometown of Athens. Along the way I have won the Fort Wayne Open (1955), the Greater Greensboro (1959), the Kansas City Open (1960), and "500" Festival Open (1963).

**7.** In 1973 I won a record $100,000 first prize by capturing the World Open, my only victory of that year. In fact, since joining the tour in 1959, I have never won two PGA tournaments in the same year, although my career earnings are over $1,000,000. Probably my best tournament was the 1971 Phoenix Open, where I carded a 23-under 261 to win.

**8.** My last tournament victory was the 1965 PGA championship. I turned pro in 1953 when I was 20 years old, but I didn't begin touring until 1960, the year I won the Sam Snead Festival. The Greater Seattle Open in 1961 and the Azalea the following year were other triumphs. I am a Texan, born, raised, and educated in Houston, where I still reside.

**9.** My earnings are right up there in the Top 25 for lifetime figures, with 1966 being the first year I topped the $100,000 barrier. That was the year I won the Bob Hope Classic, the Greater Greensboro and Jacksonville Opens. Back in 1956 I won the Canadian Open as an amateur, but the big titles have escaped me as a pro.

**10.** The most satisfying victory in my 20-year career came in 1967 when I beat Don Massengale by two strokes in an 18-hole playoff for the PGA championship. That wasn't my biggest year moneywise, though, since I've topped the $61,103 mark several times since then. I was off the tour for two and a half years before returning in 1975, at age 46, to win $69,034 and the San Antonio-Texas Open.

**11.** I have won 14 tournaments, ranging from the Fort Wayne Open in 1953, my first, to the Greater Milwaukee Open in 1975, my last. Along the way I have picked up checks for well over half a million dollars and was top money winner, Vardon Trophy winner, and Golfer of the Year in 1959.

## 128. College Champs

*Match these NCAA golf champions and the colleges they represented.*

1. Terry Small
2. Harvie Ward
3. Grier Jones
4. John Mahaffey
5. Hale Irwin
6. Tom Nieporte
7. R. H. Sikes
8. Bob Murphy
9. Jim Vickers
10. Curt Strange
11. Fred Wampler

a) Wake Forest
b) Florida
c) Ohio State
d) San Jose State
e) Purdue
f) Oklahoma
g) North Carolina
h) Houston
i) Arkansas
j) Colorado
k) Oklahoma State

## 129. Above Par

*Identify the golfers who hold these PGA records.*

1. A long-time touring pro, this man is the only golfer ever to win the same tournament eight different times, taking his first Greater Greensboro Open in 1938 and his eighth in 1965. Name him.

2. Who was the golfer who earned money in 72 consecutive tournaments, from the Carling Classic in September, 1955, to the Houston Invitational in February, 1958?

**3.** The most money won in a single calendar year is $353,021, in 1974. Who earned that much by winning the Bing Crosby, Phoenix, Dean Martin-Tucson, Tournament of Champions, Heritage, Westchester, World Open, and Kaiser International tourneys?

**4.** Name the only man to win the Tournament of Champions three years in a row, 1955, 1956, and 1957.

**5.** Who is the golfer who took the Texas Open, Houston Open, Baton Rouge Open, and St. Petersburg Open on successive weekends in 1952?

**6.** One man won the Bob Hope Desert Classic five times between 1960 and 1973. Who is he?

**7.** The widest margin of victory in a PGA event is 16 strokes, in the 1948 Chicago Victory National Championship. Name the winner.

**8.** Who is the golfer who birdied a record eight consecutive holes during the 1961 St. Petersburg Open?

**9.** At 20, this man became the youngest golfer ever to win a major tournament when he took the U.S. Open in 1922. Name him.

**10.** Name the golfer who won the Colonial National Invitation Tournament five times between 1946 and 1959.

**11.** In the 1966 Portland Open, who set a PGA record with only 102 putts during the four-round tournament?

**12.** Mike Souchak's 257 during the 1955 Texas Open is the all-time low PGA tournament score. The second lowest total is 259, achieved by which golfer who shot 62-68-63-66 in the 1945 Seattle Open?

**13.** The Vardon Trophy goes to the golfer with the lowest average in PGA events each year (minimum of 80 rounds). Who is the only man to win the Vardon Trophy three years running, 1970-72?

**14.** To make the tour, a young golfer must pass a PGA-sponsored qualifying school. In 1975, the low qualifier at the fall school was the same man who less than eight months later won the U.S. Open. Name him.

**15.** What touring pro was NCAA champion, or co-champion, three consecutive years, 1971-73, while representing the University of Texas?

**16.** Several men have won a tournament three straight years, but only one has ever won two different tournaments three times in a row. Name the winner of the Texas Open, 1960-62, and the Phoenix Open, 1961-63.

**17.** Who was the golfer who shot an all-time record low for any PGA event when he fired a 189 on the final 54 holes of the 1954 Texas Open?

**18.** Name the six golfers with 51 or more tournament victories.

# BOWLING

## 130. Right Up Your Alley

**1.** What bowling Hall of Famer nicknamed "Bloop" rolled the first 300-game in ABC Master final play in 1962; was a member of the Ziern Antiques team of St. Louis that included Don Carter, Tom Hennessey, and Pat Patterson; and was on the *Bowling* magazine first team All-America five straight years, 1959-63?

**2.** Which Hall of Famer was the first bowler to score a grand slam by winning the All-Star, World's Invitational, PBA National championship, and the ABC Masters in 1961?

**3.** This Hall of Famer, the youngest man ever voted in when he was elected at age 41 in 1970, won more than 24 PBA titles and more than $525,000. Name him.

**4.** Who was the Italian-born trick shot artist who made several bowling films during his long career, which included a victory in the 1947 All-Star tournament when he was 55 years old?

**5.** Who is the Cleveland, Ohio, bowler who owns a share of the all-time doubles record set in 1953, and was winning tournament titles from 1947 to 1961, including the 1955 and 1956 All-Star crowns?

**6.** Another Hall of Famer who made a name in exhibition and match game tours, this bowler was a member of the ABC Tournament champion Falstaffs in 1956 after taking the all-events singles title eight years earlier. Who is he?

**7.** Although a proficient bowler (member of the Knudsten all-events championship team in the 1948 ABC tournament) this Hall of Famer gained most of his fame as a bowling writer, using the Milwaukee *Journal* as a base of operations. Name him.

**8.** A member of the powerful E&B/Pfieffer team of the late 1940s and 1950s, who is the Hall of Famer who won $75,000 for rolling six consecutive strikes on the Jackpot Bowling television show in the early 1960s?

**9.** A Texan who made his mark in Chicago with teams sponsored by Tavern Pale, Jockey Cooper, and Falstaff, which bowler was twice elected Bowler of the Year, in 1945 and 1947?

**10.** An Irishman who gained fame in New York before moving to the midwest, this Hall of Fame bowler had eight sanctioned 300 games, won the ABC singles title in 1947, and was selected Bowler of the Year in 1950. Who is he?

# HORSE RACING

## 131. Long Shots

*Many so-called superhorses have been beaten on a given day. Can you name their conquerors?*

**1.** The year was 1919 and Man o' War was beaten for the only time in his life in the Sanford Stakes. Who beat him?

**2.** Canonero was trying for the Triple Crown in 1971, but after his Kentucky Derby and Preakness triumphs, a long shot beat him in the Belmont Stakes. Name that long shot.

**3.** In 1973, Secretariat was considered by many to be the "Horse of the Century," but he was beaten in the Whitney Stakes at Saratoga by what Hobeau Farm horse?

**4.** Strange things happen in the Kentucky Derby, but none could be stranger than the victory in 1913 which earned a $2 bettor $184.90. Who was this longest shot ever, upsetting Ten Point?

**5.** Riva Ridge carried the Meadow Stable silks to victory in two of the Triple Crown races, but a wet track and a Maryland-bred horse were his undoing in the Preakness. Name the horse who beat him.

## 132. Around the Oval

*Match these famous horse races with the tracks where they are run.*

1. Kentucky Derby
2. Preakness
3. Washington (D.C.) International
4. California Derby
5. American Derby
6. Louisiana Derby
7. Flamingo
8. Florida Derby
9. Colonial Cup
10. Blue Grass Stakes
11. California Stakes
12. Tri-State Futurity
13. Strub Stakes
14. Coaching Club American Oaks
15. Travers
16. Sapling Stakes
17. Jersey Derby
18. Matchmaker
19. Swift Stakes
20. Arkansas Derby

a) Fair Grounds
b) Gulfstream Park
c) Keeneland
d) Shenandoah Downs
e) Belmont Park
f) Monmouth
g) Atlantic City
h) Churchill Downs
i) Laurel
j) Arlington Park
k) Camden (S.C.)
l) Aqueduct
m) Garden State
n) Pimlico
o) Golden Gate
p) Hialeah
q) Hollywood Park
r) Oaklawn
s) Saratoga
t) Santa Anita

## 133. Triple Crown

*Sir Barton was the first horse to win the Triple Crown of thoroughbred horse racing. Who was the jockey aboard him?*

a) Isaac Murphy
b) Ted Atkinson
c) Johnny Loftus

# AUTO RACING

## 134. Behind the Wheel

**1.** Who was the race car driver who won three championship races in 1946, while no one else was winning more than one, as he took the 100-mile tests at Langhorne, Milwaukee, and Indianapolis?

**2.** In his Leader Card Special, who was the Indy 500 winner in 1962 who also accounted for the abbreviated Trenton 200, Milwaukee 200, and Syracuse 100?

**3.** Although the big one at Indianapolis escaped his grasp in 1951, this all-time driving great won more than half the championship tests that year in his Belanger Motors Special. Name him.

**4.** Who won the 100-mile race at Langhorne, Pa., in 1961, 1963, and 1964, as well as one of the two 1962 events, driving a different car each time?

**5.** Although he didn't win any other major races during the span, this driver took the Indy 500 back to back in 1953-54. Name him.

# 135. Sports Car Circuits

**1.** Who won the first Sebring Grand Prix of Endurance, back in 1952?

**2.** Who has won the Daytona 500 five times, more than anyone else?

**3.** Who won the inaugural U.S. Formula I Grand Prix in 1959 at Sebring in a Cooper-Climax?

**4.** Who won the first U.S. Grand Prix at Watkins Glen in 1961 in a Lotus-Climax?

**5.** Who won the last Grand Prix on the old 2.3-mile Watkins Glen course in a Lotus in 1970?

**6.** What internationally known playboy drove one of the Lancias in 1954 at Sebring?

**7.** Who was the "old man of racing" who won the Sebring test two years running, 1956 and 1957, with different partners?

**8.** The first race called a U.S. Grand Prix was at Riverside, Cal., in 1958. The winner drove a Scarab and the runner-up was in a Ferrari. Name the drivers.

**9.** Who won the U.S. Grand Prix at Riverside in 1960, driving a Lotus Climax?

**10.** The 1955 Sebring finishers were only 10 seconds apart. The second-place finishers were Phil Hill and Carroll Shelby in a Ferrari 750S. Who beat them in a D-type Jaguar?

# MIXED BAG

## 136. Female Firsts

**1.** Who was the first woman to play in an NCAA-sanctioned varsity basketball game when she did it with Pratt Institute?

**2.** Who was the first woman to ride in the Kentucky Derby?

**3.** Who was the first woman to drive in an USAC-sanctioned auto race?

**4.** Who was the first woman licensed to ride in a thoroughbred horse race in the U.S.?

**5.** Name the first American woman to win an Olympic sprint championship, back in 1928.

**6.** What swimmer was the first woman to win the Sullivan Trophy as America's best amateur athlete of 1944?

**7.** Who was the first woman to swim the English Channel?

## 137. Breaking the Barrier

*Track and field has had a number of "psychological barriers," such as four minutes in the mile and seven feet in the high jump. Identify the athletes who broke such barriers.*

**1.** Who was the first man to run a mile in less than four minutes?

**2.** Who broke the 60-foot mark in the shot put?

3. Who was the first man to surpass seven feet in the high jump?

4. Name the first 15-foot pole vaulter.

5. Who was the first 16-foot pole vaulter?

6. Who raised the pole vault record above 17 feet?

7. Who was the first man to exceed 29 feet in the long jump?

8. What Stanford runner was the first man to run a half mile in less than 1 minute, 50 seconds?

## 138. Speedboats

*Match the drivers or owners of the power boats on the left and the craft with which they won championships or set world records.*

1. Gar Wood
2. Herbert Mendelson
3. Mira Slovak
4. Bob Hayward
5. Jack Regas
6. Bill Stead
7. Bill Muncey
8. Lou Fageol
9. Ron Musson
10. Bill Brow

a) *Hawaii Kai*
b) *Miss Thriftway*
c) *Miss Bardahl*
d) *Miss America*
e) *Notre Dame*
f) *Miss Exide*
g) *Slo-Mo-Shun*
h) *Tahoe Miss*
i) *Miss Supertest*
j) *Maverick*

## 139. Railroad Men

1. What Chicago Bear halfback of the 1930s was known as Big Train?

2. Who was the fastballing Washington Senator pitcher called The Big Train?

3. While he played with expansion teams like the New York Mets and San Diego Padres, this Choo-Choo was a fan favorite. Name him.

4. What Hall of Fame pitcher entertained national television audiences a generation after he quit playing by singing "The Wabash Cannonball" in the broadcast booth when things got slow on the field?

5. What Choo-Choo led North Carolina to football fame in the late 1940s?

6. This Night Train was a thief who established an NFL record for pass interceptions. Name him.

7. The first iron horse was a steam engine, but who was the Iron Horse who played baseball?

# 140. Ignominy

*Some athletes achieve fame because they were in the wrong place at the right time . . . or was it the right place at the wrong time? Whatever, do you remember*

**1.** Who threw Henry Aaron his 715th career home run to break Babe Ruth's record?

**2.** When Wilt Chamberlain scored 100 points in an NBA game March 2, 1962, who were the Knicks who were supposed to be guarding him?

**3.** Who was the Montreal goaltender when Phil Esposito achieved all-time records of 76 goals and 152 points for the 1971 season?

**4.** Who is the only man to have committed—and be called for—eight personal fouls in a single regulation-time NBA game?

**5.** What Detroit pitcher was on the mound when 3-foot, 7-inch Eddie Gaedel was sent up to pinch-hit for the St. Louis Browns, August 14, 1951?

**6.** Who was the Alabama player who tackled Rice's Dickie Moegle in the 1956 Sugar Bowl?

# 141. Name Tags

**1.** What race car driver, winner of the Indianapolis 500, was known as both "The Flying Texan" and "The Houston Hustler"?

**2.** What Green Bay Packer, star of the 1930s, was called "The Hobo Halfback"?

**3.** Who was the jockey known as "Gentleman John"?

**4.** What pro golfer was often referred to as "The Silver Scot"?

**5.** What Arkansas-bred race horse of the early 1970s, who earned $846,749 dollars, was called "The Arkansas Traveler" because he would go to any track in the country to race?

**6.** What college and pro football star of the 1920s had a few nicknames, including "The Wheaton Iceman"?

**7.** What college football coach, who had played at Tennessee and in the NFL, wrestled professionally under the appellation "The Tennessee Cannonball"?

## 142. Ring a Bell?

*Match these championship performers of the 1950s with the sports in which they excelled.*

1. Tony DeSpirito
2. Hayes Jenkins
3. Bob Clotworthy
4. Art Larsen
5. Bill Muncey
6. Tommy Kono
7. Ken Henry

8. Sim Iness
9. Sam Hanks
10. Johnny Saxton
11. Tom Hennessey
12. Irving Crane
13. Jack Fleck
14. Eddie Feigner

a) Diving
b) Power boat racing
c) Speed skating
d) Auto racing
e) Bowling
f) Golf
g) Thoroughbred horse racing
h) Softball
i) Billiards
j) Figure skating
k) Tennis
l) Weightlifting
m) Track & field
n) Boxing

## 143. Food for Thought

*Sports slang takes many strange forms, including the language of the kitchen. Match the items on the left with their sports meaning on the right.*

1. Hot dog
2. Can of corn
3. Piece of cake

4. Cherry picking
5. Pickle
6. Icing
7. Rhubarb
8. Turnover
9. Turkey
10. Hamburgers
11. Western roll

12. Aspirin

13. Catching a crab
14. In the corn
15. Bagel job

a) Miss an oar stroke
b) High jump style
c) Three straight bowling strikes
d) Argument
e) Fast ball
f) Easy task
g) Show off
h) Playing the outfield
i) Baseball rundown
j) Easy to catch fly ball
k) Basket hanging in basketball
l) Sending the puck the length of the rink
m) Ballhandling mistake
n) A 6-0 set in tennis
o) Reserves

## 144. Streaks

**1.** Who was the golfer who, in the 1940s, finished in the money in a record 113 consecutive tournaments?

**2.** What hockey goalie who played with Detroit and Chicago appeared in 502 consecutive games, playing every minute of each game?

**3.** What Boston Celtic had a string of 109 consecutive playoff games in which he appeared?

**4.** Expansion teams often run into difficulties trying to win games in their formative years, yet the longest losing streak in modern baseball belongs to an old, established club. What team set the mark with 23 consecutive losses?

**5.** When Lou Gehrig was en route to his record 2,130 consecutive games played, he broke the old mark of 1,307 which had been set by a Yankee shortstop who was a teammate of Gehrig's for a while. Whose record did Gehrig break?

**6.** Archie Griffin, Ohio State's two-time Heisman Trophy winner, rushed for 100 yards or more in 22 straight games. Which team stopped his streak, and when?

**7.** Who broke up Carl Hubbell's string of consecutive strikeouts in the 1934 All-Star Game, after the National League ace had fanned Babe Ruth, Lou Gehrig, Jimmy Foxx, Al Simmons, and Joe Cronin in order?

## 145. Stars of the 1940s

*Match these champions who held their titles during the 1940s with the sports in which they reigned.*

1. Jack Adams
2. George Robson
3. Debs Garms
4. Freddie "Red" Cochrane
5. Joe Weatherly
6. Herb Mendelson
7. Art Gallagher
8. Harry Lindbergh
9. Andrew Ponzi
10. Frank Parker
11. Charles Cue

a) Speed roller skating
b) Powerboat racing
c) Boxing
d) Horse racing
e) Golf
f) Tennis
g) Auto racing
h) Pocket billiards
i) Baseball
j) Motorcycle racing
k) Rowing

## 146. A Vicious Cycle

*The six-day bicycle races were as much a part of the Depression era as were bread lines, Busby Berkeley musicals, and fireside chats. Match the partners and the years they won team championships.*

1. Georgetti
2. Kilian
3. Peden
4. Walthour
5. Letourner
6. Moretti

a) McNamera (1932)
b) Guimbretiere (1931)
c) DeBaets (1929)
d) Yates (1939)
e) Vopel (1938)
f) Crossley (1936)

## 147. Trademarks

*Several sports figures are noted for certain "trademarks," usually articles of clothing or objects carried on the bench while coaching. Match these coaches and their "trademarks."*

1. Ed Diddle
2. Red Auerbach
3. Woody Hayes
4. Hank Stram

a) Cigar
b) Vest
c) Towel
d) Shirtsleeves

## 148. Wild Men

1. Who was the Wild Bull of the Pampas?
2. Who was the Wild Horse of the Osage?

## 149. Schools for Sprinting

*Match the dash men, left, with the colleges they attended.*

1. Ray Norton
2. Charlie Greene
3. Bob Hayes
4. Dave Sime
5. Bobby Morrow
6. Lindy Ramigino
7. Harrison Dillard
8. Eddie Hart
9. Herb Washington
10. Ira Murchison

a) Western Michigan
b) California
c) Manhattan
d) San Jose State
e) Michigan State
f) Baldwin-Wallace
g) Nebraska
h) Abilene Christian
i) Florida A&M
j) Duke

# 150. Stars of the 1960s

*Identify the sports in which these personalities held championships or won titles during the 1960s.*

1. Linda Metheny
2. Diane White
3. Eddie Neloy
4. Dean Oliver
5. Allen Coage
6. Darlene Hard
7. Pete Runnels
8. Don Buse
9. Sandra Spuzich
10. Nick Werkman
11. Kiki Cutter
12. Tom Ferrell
13. Jim Phillips

14. Scott Allen
15. Larry Kristoff
16. Lones Wigger
17. Luther Lassiter
18. Billy Welu
19. Ted Turner
20. Mike Burton
21. Gary Gubner
22. Flash Elorde
23. Steve Pauley
24. Bob Gaiters
25. Larry Brown
26. Jim Rathmann

a) Judo
b) Harness horse racing
c) College basketball
d) Track
e) Figure skating
f) Skiing
g) Yachting
h) Weightlifting
i) Decathlon
j) Pro basketball
k) Auto racing
l) Gymnastics
m) Thoroughbred horse racing
n) Baseball
o) Golf
p) Billiards
q) Pro football
r) Wrestling
s) College football
t) Boxing
u) Speed skating
v) Rodeo
w) Tennis
x) Rifle shooting
y) Bowling
z) Swimming

## 151. Numbers Game

**1.** Oscar Robertson wore uniform No. 12 in college and was No. 14 with the Cincinnati Royals, but when he was traded to the Milwaukee Bucks, what number was he assigned?

**2.** Rick Barry was a baseball star in high school and his hero was Willie Mays. Barry took Mays' uniform number as his own and wore it throughout his college and pro career. What is the number?

**3.** What uniform number did Jerry West, Leroy Kelly, and Henry Aaron have in common?

**4.** The New York Yankees have retired more uniform numbers than any other baseball team. Who wore these numbers: 3, 4, 5, 7, 8 (two different men), 16, and 37?

**5.** In 1963, the most valuable players in the NFL and both major leagues of baseball all wore the same uniform number. What was the number and who were the players?

**6.** Who were the two great running backs who wore 76 and 77?

## 152. On the Prowl

*Several college teams which have achieved prominence bear the nickname "Wildcats." Identify the following.*

**1.** These Wildcats have won more national basketball titles than anyone other than UCLA.

**2.** Though a small school, the Wildcats from this college have come to attention in many sports, including track and field, with the likes of Olympic sprint champion Bobby Morrow.

**3.** Which school from the old Yankee Conference whose teams reached the NCAA football playoffs were represented by Wildcats?

**4.** Many standout athletes including Otto Graham were Wildcats at what school?

**5.** A small men's college in the South, the Wildcats from what school have been ranked among the top 20 basketball teams more than once?

**6.** A small college football power, these Wildcats were Division II NCAA champions in 1975.

**7.** Basketball, with performers like Willie Sojourner, was the road to glory for what Wildcats?

**8.** A track and field power, these Wildcats have also been a consistent winner in basketball over the years.

**9.** Who were the Wildcats who dominated the old Border Conference?

**10.** Which Wildcats are Big Eight members?

# 153. On Cue

*Which of these men was not a billiards champion?*

   a) Ralph Greenleaf
   b) Irving Crane
   c) Ike Lassiter
   d) Rudolph Wanderone

## 154. NCAA Champs

*Match these NCAA track and field champions of the last two decades with their events and schools.*

1. Frank Budd
2. Adolph Plummer
3. John Bork
4. Gerry Lindgren
5. Jerry Tarr
6. Ralph Mann
7. Sid Sink
8. Otis Burrell
9. Jan Johnson
10. Randy Matson

A 880
B) High Hurdles
C) Steeplechase
D) High Jump
E) Shot put
F) 100 Yards
G) 440
H) Pole vault
I) 6 miles
J) 440 hurdles

a) Texas A&M
b) Nevada
c) Bowling Green
d) Villanova
e) Western Michigan
f) Kansas
g) New Mexico
h) Washington St.
i) Brigham Young
j) Oregon

# ANSWERS

# 1.

1. Bobby Bonds, San Francisco, 1968
2. Chuck Hiller, San Francisco, 1962; Ken Boyer, St. Louis, 1964
3. Dave McNally, Baltimore, 1970
4. Tony Cloninger, Atlanta, 1966
5. Ernie Banks, Cubs, 1955; Jim Gentile, Baltimore, 1961
6. Ron Northey, Cardinals and Cubs; Rich Reese, Twins; Willie McCovey, Giants and Padres
7. Ray Narleski
8. Ned Garver
9. Lee "Buck" Ross

# 2.

1. Jim Perry
2. Walter Johnson
3. Warren Spahn
4. Paul Foytack
5. Jackie Jensen
6. Ty Cobb
7. Willie Stargell
8. Bobby Doerr, 1947 and 1949; Carl Yastrzemski, 1962 and 1964; Frank Howard, 1969 and 1971; George Scott, 1966, 1974, and 1975 (tied)
9. Robin Roberts
10. Willie Mays
11. Jack Billingham

## 3.

1. Bullet Joe Bush
2. Carl Scheib
3. Al Kaline, 21, Detroit, 1955
4. Pete Reiser, 22, 1941
5. Tony Conigliaro
6. Johnny Bench, 24, 1970

## 4.

1. False
2. False
3. True
4. False
5. False
6. True
7. False
8. False
9. True
10. True
11. False
12. True
13. False
14. True
15. False
16. True
17. False
18. True
19. False
20. True
21. False
22. False
23. True
24. True
25. False

## 5.

1-f, 2-g, 3-i, 4-c, 5-l, 6-k, 7-a, 8-e, 9-h, 10-b, 11-j, 12-d

## 6.

1. Jimmy Dykes
2. Eddie Sawyer
3. Joe McCarthy, Yogi Berra, Alvin Dark
4. Dick Williams
5. Fred Haney
6. Charlie Dressen, Bob Swift, Frank Skaff
7. Walter Alston
8. Roger Peckinpaugh
9. Casey Stengel, New York Mets
10. Pittsburgh, Danny Murtagh
11. Chicago White Sox, Philadelphia A's, Baltimore Orioles, Detroit Tigers, Cleveland Indians

## 7.

1. Bill Singer
2. Bill Terry
3. Bill Bruton
4. Bill Rigney
5. Bill Tuttle
6. Bill Voiselle
7. Bill Monbouquette, Boston, 1962; Bill Singer, Dodgers, 1970; Bill Stoneman, Montreal, 1969 and 1972
8. Billy Pierce
9. Bill Klem
10. Bill Hands, Chicago Cubs, 1969; Bill Singer, California, 1973
11. Bill Virdon, St. Louis, 1955
12. Bill Melton, White Sox, 1971; Bill Nicholson, Cubs, 1943 and 1944
13. Bill Lee, Cubs
14. Bill Bonham
15. Bill Jacobson

## 8.

1. Joe DiMaggio
2. Vic Wertz
3. Johnny Bench

## 9.

1. Rudy York
2. Felix Mantilla was safe on an error; Joe Adcock doubled for the first and only hit
3. Leo Durocher
4. Cookie Lavagetto
5. Lou Johnson
6. Dale Mitchell

## 10.

1. Lefty Grove, American League; Frankie Frisch, National League
2. Bob Elliott, Boston, 1947; Henry Aaron, Milwaukee, 1957
3. Ernie Banks, Chicago, 1958-59; Joe Morgan, Cincinnati, 1975-76
4. Of existing franchises, only Milwaukee, Kansas City, California, Seattle, and Toronto. The Seattle Pilots, the A's in Kansas City, and the two Washington Senator teams also failed to have an MVP.
5. New York Mets, San Diego Padres, Montreal Expos, Houston Astros, Atlanta Braves
6. Harmon Killebrew, Zoilo Versalles
7. Charlie Gehringer, Detroit, 1937; Joe Gordon, New York Yankees, 1942; Nellie Fox, Chicago White Sox, 1959; Frankie Frisch, St. Louis Cardinals, 1931; Jackie Robinson, Brooklyn, 1949; Joe Morgan, Cincinnati, 1975-76
8. Frank Robinson, Cincinnati and Baltimore
9. Jimmy Foxx, Philadelphia and Boston
10. Elston Howard, Yankees, 1963

## 11.

1. Wee Willie Keeler
2. Mike Gonzalez
3. Yogi Berra
4. Dizzy Dean
5. Casey Stengel
6. Bill Klem

## 12.

1. George Kell
2. Johnny Mize
3. Ernie Lombardi
4. Mickey Vernon
5. Eddie Mathews
6. Chuck Klein

## 13.

1-K-f; 2-D-j; 3-F-g; 4-H-k; 5-J-h; 6-L-l; 7-N-a; 8-P-m; 9-O-b; 10-M-n; 11-B-c; 12-I-o; 13-G-d; 14-E-p; 15-C-e; 16-A-i

## 14.

1. Bill Nicholson
2. Ted Williams
3. Joe Morgan, Cincinnati
4. Henry Aaron
5. Houston: Dave Roberts (5), J. R. Richard (11), Wayne Granger (2); San Francisco: John D'Acquisto (9), John Montefusco (3), Tommy Toms (3), Randy Moffitt (2)

## 15.

1. Houston Astros, San Diego Padres, Pittsburgh Pirates, Milwaukee Braves
2. Oakland, Milwaukee, California, Seattle, Toronto
3. Walt Dropo, Red Sox; Chris Chambliss, Cleveland; Mike Hargrove, Texas; Jackie Robinson, Brooklyn; Orlando Cepeda, San Francisco; Willie McCovey, San Francisco
4. Thurman Munson, New York Yankees; Johnny Bench, Cincinnati; Earl Williams, Atlanta
5. Tom Seaver, New York Mets
6. Harry Byrd
7. Albie Pearson, Bob Allison
8. Jackie Robinson, Don Newcombe, Joe Black, and Junior Gilliam, all in Brooklyn; Frank Howard, Jim Lefebvre, and Ted Sizemore in Los Angeles
9. Wally Moon, St. Louis
10. Gil MacDougald, Bob Grim, Tony Kubek, Tom Tresh, Stan Bahnsen, Thurman Munson
11. Lloyd Waner, Pittsburgh
12. LeRoy "Satchel" Paige, Cleveland

## 16.

1. Hack Wilson, Ralph Kiner, Willie Mays, Johnny Mize
2. Ralph Kiner, 1946
3. Gavvy Cravath, Philadelphia
4. Stan Musial
5. Pete Rose, Cincinnati; Ellis Burton, Chicago; Jim Russell, Boston and Brooklyn
6. Duke Snider, 1956
7. Eddie Mathews
8. Ralph Kiner
9. Willie Mays, August, 1965
10. Nate Colbert and Stan Musial

## 17.

1-d, 2-e, 3-f, 4-a, 5-b, 6-c

## 18.

1-c, 2-e, 3-d, 4-f, 5-a, 6-b

## 19.

1. Cincinnati; Bucky Walters and Paul Derringer
2. Ferguson Jenkins, Gaylord Perry, Andy Messersmith, Bill Singer
3. Urban Faber, Claude Williams, Dickie Kerr, and Eddie Cicotte
4. 1944; Detroit's Hal Newhouser and Paul "Dizzy" Trout
5. Dizzy Dean, 1934; Denny McLain, 1968

## 20.

1-c, 2-e or g, 3-e or g, 4-f, 5-h, 6-b, 7-a, 8-d

## 21.

1. Don Newcombe
2. Tom Seaver, Sandy Koufax, Jim Palmer, Denny McLain, Bob Gibson
3. Kansas City, Texas, Milwaukee, Seattle, Toronto
4. Mike Marshall, 1974
5. Houston, Montreal, Cincinnati, San Francisco
6. Dean Chance, 1964
7. Tom Seaver, 19, New York Mets, 1973; and Mike Marshall, Los Angeles, 15, 1974.
8. Denny McLain, Detroit, and Mike Cuellar, Baltimore
9. Jim Lonborg, Boston, and Mike McCormick, San Francisco
10. Early Wynn, 1959

## 22.

b, d, and e

## 23.

1. Lou Brock, Bill Bruton, Davey Lopes, Willie Mays, Bobby Tolan, Maury Wills
2. Eddie Collins, A's and White Sox; Lou Brock, St. Louis Cardinals
3. Chuck Klein, Danny Murtaugh, and Richie Ashburn, respectively
4. Luis Aparicio, White Sox
5. Gus Triandos
6. Monte Irvin, 1951; Jackie Robinson, 1955; Tim McCarver, 1964
7. Vic Power, Cleveland
8. Willie Mays
9. Lou Brock, Maury Wills, Luis Aparicio, Bert Campaneris
10. Willie Davis, 32; Tommy Davis, 18; Jim Gilliam, 17; John Roseboro, 12

## 24.

1. New York Mets, 1969
2. Bill Terry, Travis Jackson, Fred Lindstrom, Mel Ott, Freddy Leach, Shanty Hogan, Bob O'Farrell, Doc Marshall, Ethan Allen
3. Showboat Fisher, George Watkins, Gus Mancuso, Frankie Frisch, Chick Hafey, Jim Bottomley, Charlie Gilbert, Sparky Adams, Taylor Douthit, Jimmie Wilson
4. Norm Cash and Al Kaline
5. Danny Cater
6. Ted Williams and Vern Stephens
7. Roy White
8. Charlie Gehringer
9. Tom Tresh
10. Bobby Richardson, Bill Skowron, Tony Kubek, Mickey Mantle, Bob Cerv, Elston Howard, Johnny Blanchard, Hector Lopez

## 25.

1. Frank Thomas in left, Earl Smith in center
2. Yogi Berra, 87 games; Hector Lopez, 72
3. Enos Slaughter, Stan Musial, Terry Moore
4. Del Ennis, Richie Ashburn, Dick Sisler
5. Babe Ruth, Earle Combs, Ben Chapman
6. Henry Aaron (14), Wes Covington (14), Andy Pafko (10), Bill Bruton (7), Bob Hazle (4)
7. Adam Comorosky, Woody Jensen
8. Mickey Mantle, Hank Bauer, Gene Woodling
9. Bobby Veach
10. Dom DiMaggio, Lou Finney

## 26.

1. Rogers Hornsby, Hack Wilson, Mel Ott, Chuck Klein, Joe Medwick, Tommy Davis
2. Orlando Cepeda, San Francisco Giants
3. Dick Allen, 1972
4. Rogers Hornsby, St. Louis; George Kelly, New York Giants
5. Lou Gehrig, Joe DiMaggio, Tony Lazzeri, George Selkirk, Bill Dickey

## 27.

1. George Kell
2. Babe Dahlgren
3. Charlie Silvera
4. Carroll Hardy, 1960

## 28.

1. Henry Chadwick
2. Bugs Baer
3. Ernest Thayer
4. Oliver Hazard Perry Cuyler
5. Byron Bancroft "Ban" Johnson
6. Franklin P. Adams
7. Ford Frick

## 29.

1. Bill Melton
2. Jim Gentile, 1961
3. Tommy Harper, Boston and Seattle/Milwaukee
4. Ty Cobb, Al Kaline, Harry Heilmann, Charlie Gehringer, Sam Crawford, Hank Greenberg, Norm Cash, Bobby Veach
5. Babe Ruth
6. Dom DiMaggio
7. Earl Averill, Hal Trosky, Larry Doby
8. Babe Ruth, Lou Gehrig, Earl Coombs, Joe DiMaggio, Bill Dickey, Bob Meusel, Ben Chapman
9. Ed Brinkman
10. Tony Oliva, Harmon Killebrew, Rod Carew, Cesar Tovar, Zoilo Versalles, Bob Allison

## 30.

1. New York
2. Pittsburgh
3. Philadelphia
4. Detroit
5. St. Louis
6. Cincinnati
7. Brooklyn
8. Houston
9. Boston
10. San Francisco
11. Seattle
12. Washington
13. Los Angeles

## 31.

1. Rogers Hornsby: .424 with the Cardinals, .387 with the Braves, .380 with the Cubs
2. Rusty Staub: .333 with Houston, .311 with Montreal
3. Joe Medwick, 1937
4. Rabbit Maranville
5. Mel Ott
6. Honus Wagner, Roberto Clemente, Pie Traynor, Willie Stargell, Paul Waner
7. Del Ennis
8. Tommy Holmes, 1945
9. Frank Chance, 1903
10. Ken Boyer

## 32.

1. Roy Campanella, Ted Kluszewski, Eddie Mathews, Duke Snider
2. Darrell Evans, Davey Johnson, Henry Aaron
3. Eddie Mathews
4. Enos Slaughter, Cardinals/Yankees; Roger Maris, Yankees/Cardinals; Frank Robinson, Reds/Orioles; Bill Skowron, Yankees/Dodgers
5. Joe Cronin, 1943
6. Jerry Lynch, Cincinnati and Pittsburgh
7. Jim Perry, Cleveland; Frank Lary, Detroit; George "Pete" Burnside, Washington

## 33.

1. Phil Regan
2. Bill Skowron
3. Leon Goslin
4. Walter Maranville
5. John Jorgenson
6. Joe Medwick
7. Charlie Keller, Dave Kingman
8. Duke Snider
9. Ken Harrelson, Bob Taylor
10. George Haas
11. Ron Cey
12. Jim Grant
13. Mike Garcia
14. Orlando Cepeda
15. Doug Rader

## 34.

a, f, g, j

# 35.

1. Los Angeles Angels and Washington Senators
2. Bill Rigney, Los Angeles; Mickey Vernon, Washington
3. Eli Grba, New York Yankee relief pitcher, by Los Angeles
4. Bobby Shantz, pitcher, also from the Yankees
5. Harry Craft, Colt 45s; Casey Stengel, Mets
6. San Francisco Giants
7. Ed Bressoud, Houston; Hobie Landrith, New York
8. Al Spangler, Houston; Lee Walls, New York
9. Bobby Shantz, Washington from the Yankees and Houston from the Pirates
10. Jim Fregosi, Ed Brinkman, Claude Osteen
11. Ed Kranepool, Dave Giusti
12. Montreal Expos, Gene Mauch; San Diego Padres, Preston Gomez; Kansas City Royals, Joe Gordon; Seattle Pilots, Joe Schultz
13. Ollie Brown, San Diego
14. Manny Mota, by Montreal from Pittsburgh
15. Roger Nelson, by Kansas City from Baltimore; Don Mincher, by Seattle from California
16. Angels were 86-76, .531 in their second season of 1962
17. Kansas City, 1971
18. Clarence Gaston
19. Chicago Cubs

## 36.

1. Jon Matlack
2. Randy Gumpert
3. Chicago
4. Boston Red Sox
5. John Stephenson
6. Casey Stengel
7. Oscar Gamble
8. Red Ruffing
9. Warren Spahn
10. Rich Reese

## 37.

1-c, 2-d, 3-e, 4-b, 5-a

## 38.

1. Willie Jones
2. Vernal "Nippy" Jones
3. Sad Sam "Toothpick" Jones
4. Sherman "Roadblock" Jones
5. Mack "the Knife" Jones
6. Dalton Jones
7. Bob "Ducky" Jones

## 39.

1. Bill Melton, 1971; Dick Allen, 1972
2. Wally Pipp, 1916; Graig Nettles, 1976
3. Eddie Yost, 12; Mickey Vernon, 10; Jackie Jensen, 10
4. Al Kaline
5. Roy Sievers, 1957
6. Roger Maris, Babe Ruth, Jimmy Foxx, Hank Greenberg, Mickey Mantle
7. 22, Nick Etten, New York, 1944
8. 54, Mickey Mantle, 1961
9. Frank Howard, the "new" Washington Senators, 1968
10. Bill Skowron, 28; Yogi Berra, 21; Elston Howard, 21; Johnny Blanchard, 21

## 40.

1. George Blanda
2. Mike Clark
3. Dan Pastorini
4. Len Dawson
5. MacArthur Lane
6. Tommy Wade
7. Roman Gabriel (96, at start of '76)
8. Otto Graham, Sam Etcheverry, and Roman Gabriel, respectively
9. Ron Smith, Ron Meyer, Amos Bullocks
10. Frank Sinkwich
11. Eddie LeBaron
12. Roger Staubach, 1976
13. Earl Morrall, Baltimore; Craig Morton, Dallas; Billy Kilmer, Washington; Fran Tarkenton, Minnesota

## 41.

1. Vernal LeVoir
2. Pat Richter
3. Bobby Joe Conrad
4. Charlie Justice
5. Pat Harder
6. Tad Weed
7. Elroy Hirsch
8. Greg Cook

## 42.

1. Tittle
2. Owens
3. Holub
4. Hicks
5. Dupre
6. Caroline
7. Boone
8. Smith or Roberts or Hill
9. Greenwood

## 43.

1. Bob Hayes
2. Ray Barbuti
3. Jim Thorpe
4. Milt Campbell
5. Glenn Davis
6. Gerald Tinker

## 44.

1. Tom Dempsey
2. Harry Gilmer
3. Dick Lane
4. Tommy O'Connell, Browns; Tommy Thompson, Eagles
5. Dick Bass
6. Tom Fears
7. Dick James
8. Tom Brown
9. Harry Jagade

## 45.

## 46.

1-l, 2-m, 3-e, 4-i, 5-j, 6-f, 7-a, 8-n or b, 9-k, 10-b or n, 11-h, 12-c, 13-g, 14-d

## 47.

1. Bills or Bisons
2. Browns
3. Colts
4. Dodgers
5. Dons
6. 49ers
7. Rockets or Hornets
8. Seahawks
9. Yankees

## 48.

1. Paul Christman, Pat Harder, Charley Trippi, Marshall Goldberg
2. Larry Csonka and Jim Kiick
3. Don Miller
4. Bob Gaiters and Pervis Atkins
5. Baseball catcher Tom Haller
6. Bert Coan and Curtis McClinton
7. Donny Anderson and Jim Grabowski
8. John Unitas, L. G. Dupre, Alan Ameche, Lenny Moore

**49.**

a

**50.**

b, d, e

**51.**

1-c, 2-d, 3-a, 4-e, 5-b

## 52.

1. Sam
2. Tuffy
3. Bake
4. Wahoo
5. Sonny
6. Cookie
7. Bart (or Bartlett)
8. Buck
9. Curly
10. Pat
11. Bucko
12. Joe
13. Scooter
14. Paddy
15. Breezy
16. Bambi
17. Pete
18. Pat
19. Barney
20. Sam
21. Doak
22. Zeke

## 53.

1. Glenn Davis
2. Milt Davis
3. Ernie Davis
4. Glenn Davis
5. Fred Davis
6. Ben Davis
7. Tommy Davis
8. Willie Davis

## 54.

1. Joe Perry
2. Joe Fortunato
3. Joe Guyon
4. Joe Kapp
5. Joe Stydahar
6. Joe Schmidt
7. Joe Arenas
8. Joe Namath
9. Joe Laws
10. Joe Muha

## 55.

1. Dave Robinson, Ray Nitschke, Lee Roy Caffey
2. Jack Ham, Jack Lambert, Andy Russell
3. Ralph Baker, Al Atkinson, Larry Grantham
4. Dave Edwards, LeRoy Jordan, Chuck Howley
5. Ray May, Mike Curtis, Ted Hendricks

## 56.

1-h, 2-m, 3-i, 4-p, 5-q, 6-r, 7-w, 8-a, 9-s, 10-x, 11-bb, 12-d, e, or t, 13-c, 14-cc, 15-y, 16-u, 17-d or e, 18-v, 19-j, 20-d, e, or t, 21-z, 22-aa, 23-f, 24-k, 25-o, 26-g, 27-l, 28-n, 29-b

# 57.

1. Indiana and Wisconsin
2. Elmer Layden
3. A-b; B-c; C-a
4. Don Hutson
5. Southern Methodist
6. Mel Anthony
7. Alabama, 1946
8. George Halas
9. Southern California 14, Penn State 3
10. Pete Beathard
11. Illinois (3), Iowa (2)
12. Southern California
13. Ron VanderKelen
14. Ohio State 17, California 14
15. John Charles
16. Ernie Nevers, Stanford, and Vic Bottari, California, respectively
17. Steve Horowitz
18. Michigan vs. Stanford, 1902; Michigan vs. Southern California, 1948
19. Bob Jeter
20. Pat Richter

# 58.

1-p, 2-i or h; 3-f, 4-a, 5-j or t; 6-k or q; 7-b, 8-1, 9-m, 10-n, 11-c or e; 12-g, 13-d or o; 14-s; 15-h or i; 16-r; 17-c or e; 18-j or t; 19-d or o; 20-q or k

## 59.

1. Crimson
2. Golden
3. Scarlet
4. Red
5. Blue
6. Maroons
7. Green
8. Blue
9. Black
10. Green
11. Blue
12. Orange
13. Golden
14. Red
15. Rainbows

## 60.

b (1937), c (1935), d (1959), g (last time, 1960), j (1953)

Source, *The Official NCAA Football Guide.*

## 61.

1. Sleepy Jim Crowley
2. Mrs. Lou Gehrig
3. Glenn Dobbs
4. Spec Sanders
5. New York, 1946 and 1947; Buffalo, 1948; San Francisco, 1949
6. Joe Perry
7. Ben Agajanian
8. Mac Speedie and Dante Lavelli
9. 1946, Lou Groza, Cleveland; 1947, Spec Sanders, New York; 1948, Chet Mutryn, Buffalo; 1949, Al Beals, San Francisco
10. a, d, e, h, i, k, m, n, o

## 62.

1-d, 2-g, 3-i, 4-l, 5-j, 6-m, 7-k, 8-c, 9-f, 10-b, 11-e, 12-a, 13-h

## 63.

1. Wisconsin, Northwestern, Michigan, Chicago, Minnesota, Illinois, Purdue, Iowa, Indiana, Ohio State, Michigan State
2. Tom Harmon
3. Mike Phipps
4. Northwestern
5. Jay Berwanger
6. Len Dawson to Erich Barnes
7. Eric "The Flea" Allen
8. Ron Johnson
9. Jim Lash
10. Jim Bakken
11. Jack Clancy

## 64.

1-c, 2-e, 3-d, 4-f, 5-a, 6-b

## 65.

1. Bubba Smith
2. Ernie Smith
3. J. Robert "Bob" Smith
4. Dave Smith
5. Nolan Smith
6. Jackie Smith
7. Bill Smith
8. Billy Ray Smith

## 66.

1-c, 2-e, 3-g, 4-h, 5-i, 6-b, 7-j, 8-a, 9-f, 10-d

## 67.

1-d, 2-g, 3-e, 4-i, 5-k, 6-a, 7-j, 8-b, 9-h, 10-c, 11-f

## 68.

1-r, 2-s, 3-a, 4-t, 5-b, 6-dd, 7-c, 8-ee, 9-d, 10-ff, 11-e, 12-w, 13-f, 14-x, 15-g, 16-y, 17-h, 18-i, 19-z, 20-j, 21-aa, 22-bb, 23-k, 24-l, 25-m, 26-gg, 27-n, 28-cc, 29-o, 30-v, 31-p, 32-u, 33-q

## 69.

1. Toronto, nicknamed the Northmen
2. J. J. Jennings, John Harvey, Willie Spencer
3. Action point
4. Greg Barton
5. Dicker-rod
6. Birmingham 22, Florida 21
7. J. J. Jennings, Memphis; Tommy Reamon, Florida; Tony Adams, Southern California
8. Billy Hobbs
9. Merle Harmon and Alex Hawkins
10. Tommy Reamon
11. Anthony Davis, Southern California Sun

## 70.

1. Vern Mikkelsen, Bob Harrison, George Mikan, Pep Saul, Slater Martin
2. Dick Barnett, Walt Frazier, Bill Bradley, Dave DeBusschere, Willis Reed
3. Bob Pettit, Cliff Hagan, Charlie Share, Slater Martin, Jack McMahon
4. Bob Cousy, Bill Sharman, Tommy Heinsohn, Jim Loscutoff
5. John Havlicek, Tom Sanders, K. C. Jones, Sam Jones
6. Jerry West, Elgin Baylor, Rudy LaRusso, Jim Krebs
7. Wilt Chamberlain, Hal Greer, Luke Jackson, Chet Walker, Wally Jones
8. Bob Davies, Arnie Risen, Bobby Wanzer, Jack Coleman, Arnie Johnson
9. Wilt Chamberlain, Happy Hairston, Gail Goodrich, Jerry West, Jim McMillian
10. Dolph Schayes, Wally Osterkorn, Earl Lloyd, Paul Seymour, Dick Farley

## 71.

| *Basketball* | *Baseball* |
|---|---|
| 1. Fort Wayne Pistons | Pittsburgh Pirates<br>St. Louis Cardinals |
| 2. Boston Celtics<br>New York Knicks | Boston/Milwaukee Braves<br>Philadelphia Phillies<br>Boston Red Sox |

3. Boston Celtics — Brooklyn Dodgers
Chicago Cubs

4. New York Knicks — Chicago White Sox
Detroit Pistons

5. Los Angeles Lakers — Chicago White Sox
San Francisco       Minnesota Twins
  Warriors
Kentucky Colonels
  (ABA)

6. Minneapolis Lakers — Cleveland Indians
Washington Senators
New York Yankees
Chicago White Sox
San Francisco Giants
Chicago Cubs

7. Detroit Pistons — Atlanta Braves
St. Louis Cardinals
Philadelphia Phillies

8. Youngstown (NBL)
Cleveland Rebels — Cincinnati Reds
  (BAA)          Chicago Cubs

9. Toronto Huskies — Philadelphia Phillies
  (BAA)
                  Philadelphia Athletics
10. St. Louis Hawks
Rochester/Cincinnati
  Royals — St. Louis Cardinals

11. Anderson Packers
  (NBL)
Fort Wayne Pistons — Brooklyn Dodgers
Minneapolis Lakers

Philadelphia Phillies
Cincinnati Reds

## 72.

1-d, 2-f, 3-h, 4-j, 5-k, 6-n, 7-l, 8-o, 9-q, 10-s, 11-a, 12-p, 13-r, 14-t, 15-m, 16-c, 17-i, 18-e, 19-g, 20-b

## 73.

1. Bob Pettit
2. Bob Cousy, 1957; Oscar Robertson, 1964
3. Jerry West
4. a
5. Bob Pettit
6. Wes Unseld, 1969
7. Ed Macauley
8. Jerry West
9. b

## 74.

1-e, 2-g, 3-k, 4-h, 5-a, 6-i, 7-b, 8-j, 9-c, 10-f, 11-d

## 75.

1. Nate Thurmond and Jerry Lucas
2. Dolph Schayes
3. Harry Gallatin and Ray Felix
4. Tom Heinsohn, 732; Gene Conley, 550; Frank Ramsey, 431; Sam Jones, 421
5. Jerry Lucas, Bob Pettit, Elgin Baylor, Dolph Schayes, Bill Bridges
6. Artis Gilmore, Kentucky Colonels
7. Spencer Heywood, Denver
8. Bob Pettit
9. Mel Daniels

## 76.

1. Al Attles and K. C. Jones, 1976
2. Jerry Fleishman played with Philadelphia from 1946 to 1953, but appeared with the New York Knicks in the 1953 playoffs.
3. Pittsburgh
4. Cleveland Pipers of the American Basketball League
5. George Hauptfuher of Harvard, by Boston
6. Wilt Chamberlain and Jack Twyman

## 77.

1-e, 2-i, 3-f, 4-j, 5-a, 6-l, 7-b, 8-m, 9-c, 10-o, 11-d, 12-n, 13-g, 14-k, 15-h

## 78.

1. Andy Phillip
2. Wilt Chamberlain
3. Rick Barry
4. Bob Pettit, Clyde Lovellette
5. Hal Greer
6. Julius Erving and Artis Gilmore, respectively
7. Gail Goodrich
8. Jerry Lucas, Jack Twyman, Adrian Smith
9. Dave Robisch and Ralph Simpson
10. Joe Ruklick

## 79.

1-g, b, and n; 2-e; 3-i; 4-l; 5-k; 6-b and n; 7-m; 8-c; 9-b and n; 10-d; 11-d and a; 12-f; 13-j; 14-h

## 80.

1-d, 2-f, 3-h, 4-j, 5-m, 6-o, 7-q, 8-s, 9-r, 10-u, 11-v, 12-x, 13-y, 14-w, 15-z, 16-t, 17-l, 18-i, 19-c, 20-e, 21-g, 22-k, 23-n, 24-a, 25-b, 26-p

## 81.

1-e, 2-j, 3-g, 4-a, 5-h, 6-k or n, 7-b, 8-n, 9-m, 10-c, 11-o, 12-i, 13-f, 14-d, 15-p, 16-l

## 82.

1-e, 2-g, 3-k, 4-f, 5-a, 6-d, 7-h, 8-b, 9-j, 10-m, 11-l, 12-i, 13-c

## 83.

1-e, 2-b, 3-g, 4-h, 5-a, 6-c, 7-d, 8-f

## 84.

1. Pete Maravich, Louisiana State; Frank Selvy, Furman; Johnny Neumann, Mississippi
2. Paul Arizin
3. Dwight "Bo" Lamar
4. Grady Wallace
5. Frank Selvy
6. Billy McGill
7. Bill Bradley
8. Nick Werkman, Seton Hall; Barry Kramer, NYU
9. Howard "Butch" Komives
10. Dickie Hemric

## 85.

1-c, 2-e, 3-d, 4-a, 5-b

## 86.

1. Park
2. Reed
3. Shectman
4. McMillon
5. Green
6. Butcher
7. Beaty
8. Rocha
9. Palazzi
10. Kimball
11. Martin
12. Murrey
13. Todorovich

## 87.

1. Cazzie Russell
2. Hank Luisetti
3. Hank Iba
4. Don Kojis
5. Tom Meschery
6. Larry Brown
7. Frank Lubin
8. Don Barksdale and Davage Minor
9. Bob Kurland
10. Dick Boushka

## 88.

1-d, 2-g, 3-e, 4-a, 5-h, 6-b, 7-f, 8-c

## 89.

1. Long Island, New York
2. Abe Saperstein
3. John McLendon, Cleveland
4. Connie Hawkins
5. Kansas City
6. b, c, d, g

## 90.

1. Babe Didrikson
2. Ben Hogan
3. Roy Campanella
4. Maurice Stokes
5. Harlem Globetrotters
6. Elroy Hirsch
7. Vince Lombardi

## 91.

1-p, 2-k, 3-i, 4-l, 5-j, 6-m, 7-h, 8-a, 9-n, 10-f, 11-o, 12-c, 13-g, 14-e, 15-d, 16-b

## 92.

1. Glenn Ford
2. James Caan
3. Billy Dee Williams
4. Errol Flynn
5. James Earl Jones
6. Alex Karras
7. Susan Clark
8. William Bendix
9. Coley Wallace
10. Greg McClure
11. Pat O'Brien
12. Paul Winfield

## 93.

1-d, 2-f, 3-e, 4-g, 5-b, 6-h, 7-a, 8-c

## 94.

1-d, 2-g, 3-n, 4-h, 5-k, 6-l, 7-m, 8-a, 9-e, 10-b, 11-f, 12-c, 13-j, 14-i

## 95.

1-d, 2-f, 3-h, 4-k, 5-a, 6-i, 7-b, 8-l, 9-c, 10-m, 11-e, 12-n, 13-j, 14-g

## 96.

1-g, 2-h, 3-a, 4-k, 5-b, 6-j, 7-l, 8-e, 9-c, 10-f, 11-d, 12-i

## 97.

a, d, f, h, j

## 98.

1. Rubin Carter
2. Archie Moore
3. Theodore "Tiger" Flowers
4. Sugar Ray Robinson
5. Archie Moore
6. Primo Carnera
7. Jess Willard
8. 29
9. Tony Zale and Billy Prior
10. Steve Hamas
11. Randy Turpin

## 99.

1-d, 2-g, 3-e, 4-h, 5-i, 6-c, 7-k, 8-b, 9-l, 10-a, 11-f, 12-j

## 100.

All lost their titles to Sugar Ray Robinson.

## 101.

1-e, 2-g, 3-i, 4-a, 5-h, 6-b, 7-j, 8-c, 9-f, 10-d

## 102.

1-j, 2-p, 3-k, 4-r, 5-l, 6-q, 7-b, 8-m, 9-s, 10-c, 11-n, 12-t, 13-d, 14-u, 15-e, 16-f, 17-v, 18-a, 19-g, 20-o, 21-h, 22-i

## 103.

1-c, 2-g, 3-f, 4-a, 5-d, 6-b, 7-e

## 104.

1-d, 2-f, 3-a, 4-h, 5-i, 6-b, 7-e, 8-c, 9-g

# 105.

1. Don Schollander
2. Charlie Daniels
3. Ford Konno, Clark Scholes, and Yoshinobu Oyakawa, respectively
4. Bill Yorzyk
5. Duke Kahanamoku
6. Frank McKinney, backstroke; Paul Hart, breaststroke; Lance Larson, butterfly; Jeff Farrell, freestyle
7. Norman Ross
8. Roland Matthes
9. Ralph Breyer, Harry Glance, Wally O'Connor
10. 100- and 200-meter freestyle; 100- and 200-meter butterfly; 4x100-meter freestyle, 4x200-meter freestyle, and 4x100-meter medley relays
11. 400-meter freestyle
12. 200-meter breaststroke, won by David Wilkie, Great Britain

# 106.

1. Germany
2. Australia
3. Canada
4. Germany
5. The Netherlands
6. Norway
7. Czechoslovakia
8. Poland
9. Canada
10. Soviet Union

## 107.

1. John and Ben Peterson
2. Henry Wittenberg
3. Terry McCann, Shelby Wilson, and Doug Bluebaugh, respectively
4. Dan Gable, Wayne Wells, and Ben Peterson, respectively
5. Chris Taylor
6. John Peterson

## 108.

1. Charles Adkins, Nathan Brooks, Norvel Lee, Floyd Patterson, Ed Sanders
2. Frank Genaro and Eddie Eagan, respectively
3. Ray Seales
4. Nino Benvenuti
5. Fidel LaBarba and Jackie Fields, respectively
6. Laszlo Papp
7. Eddie Flynn and Carmen Barth, respectively
8. Pete Rademacher
9. Victor Peralta
10. Pascual Perez
11. Light heavyweight

# 109.

1. Canada
2. Aleksandr Belov
3. Doug Collins
4. Jay Arnette, Walt Bellamy, Bob Boozer, Terry Dischinger, Burdette Haldorson, Darrall Imhoff, Al Kelley, Lester Lane, Jerry Lucas, Oscar Robertson, Adrian Smith, Jerry West
5. Bob Kurland
6. Dick Boushka, Carl Cain, Chuck Darling, Burdette Haldorson, Bill Hoagland, K. C. Jones
7. Spencer Haywood, and JoJo White and Mike Barrett
8. Jim Barnes, Larry Brown, Bill Bradley, Joe Caldwell, Mel Counts, Dick Davies, Walt Hazzard, Luke Jackson, Jeff Mullins, George Wilson

# 110.

1-h or f, 2-e, 3-g, 4-i, 5-a, 6-j, 7-b, 8-c, 9-f, 10-d

# 111.

1. Paul Anderson
2. Joe DePietro
3. Charles Vinci
4. Norb Schemansky
5. Tommy Kono

## 112.

1. Albert White
2. Pete DesJardins
3. Dr. Sammy Lee
4. Bob Webster
5. Klaus DiBiasi
6. Pat McCormick
7. Aileen Riggin and Helen Wainwright, respectively
8. Vicky Draves
9. Ingrid Kramer
10. Marjorie Gestring

## 113.

1. Horace Ashenfelter
2. Larry Black, Robert Taylor, Gerald Tinker, Eddie Hart
3. Tommie Smith and John Carlos
4. Archie Williams and John Woodruff, respectively
5. Mal Whitfield and Arthur Wint, respectively
6. Otis Davis and Glenn Davis, respectively
7. Peter Snell, New Zealand
8. Bobby Joe Morrow
9. Ralph Hill
10. Dave Wottle

# 114.

1. Wyomia Tyus
2. Mildred McDaniel
3. Jean Shiley
4. Fanny Blankers-Koen
5. Helen Stephens
6. Hammond (400 meters) and Schmidt (javelin)
7. Wyomia Tyus, Barbara Ferrell, Margaret Bailes, Mildrette Netter
8. Olga Fikotova
9. Wilma Rudolph
10. Mae Faggs, Barbara Jones, Janet Moreau, Cathy Hardy

# 115.

1. Dick Fosbury
2. DeBart Hubbard
3. Cornelius Johnson
4. Parry O'Brien
5. Bob Beamon
6. Al Oerter
7. Bob Richards
8. Jesse Owens
9. Randy Williams
10. Parry O'Brien, Darrow Hooper, and James Fuchs, respectively

## 116.

1. Chris von Saltza
2. Ethelda Bleibtry
3. Eleanor Holm Jarrett
4. Debbie Meyer
5. Helene Madison
6. Ann Curtis
7. Gertrude Ederle
8. Dawn Fraser
9. Sharon Stouder
10. Shelley Mann
11. Shane Gould

## 117.

1. Austria
2. Czechoslovakia
3. Uganda
4. Canada
5. Australia
6. Italy
7. Finland
8. Jamaica
9. Argentina
10. Ethiopia
11. Greece

# 118.

1. Ross Lonsberry, 1971-72
2. Andy Hebenton
3. Glenn Hall
4. Terry Sawchuk
5. Alex Delvecchio

# 119.

1. California Seals, Los Angeles Kings, Minnesota North Stars, Philadelphia Flyers, Pittsburgh Penguins, St. Louis Blues
2. Dave Balon, by Minnesota from Montreal
3. Philadelphia Flyers
4. St. Louis Blues
5. Philadelphia Flyers, 1974
6. Buffalo Sabres, Vancouver Canucks
7. Danny Grant, Minnesota
8. Atlanta Flames, New York Islanders
9. Bobby Clarke, 1973
10. Kansas City Scouts, Washington Capitals
11. Glenn Hall, St. Louis
12. Richard Martin, Buffalo

## 120.

1. Terry Sawchuk and Wayne Connelly, respectively
2. Ralph "Scotty" Bowman
3. George Hainsworth
4. Steve Atkinson and Nelson Pyatt


## 121.

1. Bryan Hextall
2. Phil Goyette
3. Phil Esposito, Boston, 1971-74; Gordie Howe, Detroit, 1951-54
4. Babe Pratt and Ted Kennedy, respectively
5. Stan Mikita, Chicago Black Hawks
6. Toe Blake
7. Red Kelly, Detroit; Doug Harvey, Montreal; Tom Johnson, Montreal; Pierre Pilote, Chicago; Jacques LaPerrière, Montreal; Harry Howell, New York Rangers; Bobby Orr, Boston
8. Jack Gelineau, Larry Regan, Bobby Orr, Derek Sanderson
9. Jacques Plante and Glenn Hall
10. Jean Beliveau
11. Bernie Geoffrion, 1955; Jean Beliveau, 1956; Dickie Moore, 1958-59
12. Claude Provost
13. Ed Litzenberger, Bill Hay, and Tony Esposito, respectively
14. Bobby Orr
15. Gordie Drillon

## 122.

b

## 123.

1. Bentley
2. Pronovost
3. Plager
4. Boucher
5. Cullen
6. Stanfield
7. Conacher

## 124.

1. Eddie Shore
2. Nos. 9 and 10, respectively
3. Wayne Maki
4. Jean Beliveau, Howie Morenz, and Maurice Richard, respectively
5. Bill Masterson
6. Tim Horton

## 125.

1. Dit
2. Cooney
3. Ching
4. Toe
5. Hooley
6. Butch
7. Tiny
8. Newsy
9. Moose
10. Mickey
11. Black Jack
12. Sweeney
13. Babe
14. Bullet Joe
15. Hap
16. Buck
17. Barney
18. Pit
19. Scotty
20. Babe
21. Turk
22. Shorty
23. Hap
24. Busher
25. King

## 126.

1-e, 2-h, 3-a, 4-f, 5-b, 6-i, 7-c, 8-j, 9-d, 10-g

## 127.

1. Gene Littler
2. Orville Moody
3. Tommy Aaron
4. Doug Ford
5. George Archer
6. Dow Finsterwald
7. Miller Barber
8. Dave Marr
9. Doug Sanders
10. Don January
11. Art Wall, Jr.

## 128.

1-d, 2-g, 3-k, 4-h, 5-j, 6-c, 7-i, 8-b, 9-f, 10-a, 11-e

## 129.

1. Sam Snead
2. Dow Finsterwald
3. Johnny Miller
4. Gene Littler
5. Jackie Burke, Jr.
6. Arnold Palmer
7. Bobby Locke
8. Bob Goalby
9. Gene Sarazen
10. Ben Hogan
11. Bert Yancy
12. Byron Nelson
13. Lee Trevino
14. Jerry Pate
15. Ben Crenshaw
16. Arnold Palmer
17. Chandler Harper
18. Sam Snead, Jack Nicklaus, Ben Hogan, Arnold Palmer, Byron Nelson, Billy Casper

## 130.

1. Ray Bluth
2. Don Carter
3. Dick Weber
4. Andy Varipapa
5. Steve Nagy
6. Ned Day
7. Billy Sixty
8. Therman Gibson
9. Buddy Bomar
10. Junie McMahon

## 131.

1. Upset
2. Pass Catcher
3. Onion
4. Donerail
5. Bee Bee Bee

## 132.

1-h, 2-n, 3-i, 4-o, 5-j, 6-a, 7-p, 8-b, 9-k, 10-c, 11-q, 12-d, 13-t, 14-e, 15-s, 16-f, 17-m, 18-g, 19-l, 20-r

## 133.

c

## 134.

1. Rex Mays
2. Rodger Ward
3. Tony Bettenhausen
4. A. J. Foyt
5. Bill Vukovich

## 135.

1. Harry Gray and Larry Kulok in a Frazer-Nash
2. Richard Petty
3. Bruce McLaren
4. Innes Ireland
5. Emerson Fittipaldi
6. Porforio Rubirosa
7. Juan Fangio
8. Chuck Daigh beat Dan Gurney
9. Stirling Moss
10. Mike Hawthorne and Phil Walters

## 136.

1. Cyndi Meserve
2. Diane Crump
3. Janet Guthrie
4. Kathy Kusner
5. Betty Robinson
6. Ann Curtis
7. Gertrude Ederle

## 137.

1. Roger Bannister
2. Parry O'Brien
3. Charlie Dumas
4. Cornelius Warmerdam
5. John Uelses
6. John Pennel
7. Bob Beamon
8. Ben Eastman

## 138.

1-d, 2-e, 3-h, 4-i, 5-a, 6-j, 7-b, 8-g, 9-c, 10-f

## 139.

1. Johnny Sisk
2. Walter Johnson
3. Clarence Coleman
4. Dizzy Dean
5. Charlie Justice
6. Dick Lane
7. Lou Gehrig

## 140.

1. Al Downing
2. Darrall Imhoff, Cleveland Buckner, and Willie Naulls, among others
3. Phil Myre
4. Don Otten: Tri-Cities vs. Sheboygan, November 24, 1949
5. Bob Cain
6. Tommy Lewis

## 141.

1. A. J. Foyt
2. Johnny "Blood" McNally
3. John A. Rotz
4. Tommy Armour
5. No double
6. Harold ("Red," "The Galloping Ghost") Grange
7. Herman Hickman

## 142.

1-g, 2-j, 3-a, 4-k, 5-b, 6-l, 7-c, 8-m, 9-d, 10-n, 11-e, 12-i, 13-f, 14-h

## 143.

1-g, 2-j, 3-f, 4-k, 5-i, 6-l, 7-d, 8-m, 9-c, 10-o, 11-b, 12-e, 13-a, 14-h, 15-n

## 144.

1. Byron Nelson
2. Glenn Hall
3. Bob Cousy
4. Philadelphia Phillies, 1961
5. Everett Scott's
6. Southern California, 1975 Rose Bowl
7. Bill Dickey

## 145.

1-d, 2-g, 3-i, 4-c, 5-j, 6-b, 7-k, 8-a, 9-h, 10-f, 11-e

## 146.

1-c, 2-e, 3-a, 4-f, 5-b, 6-d

## 147.

1-c, 2-a, 3-d, 4-b

## 148.

1. Luis Firpo
2. Pepper Martin

## 149.

1-d, 2-g, 3-i, 4-j, 5-h, 6-c, 7-f, 8-b, 9-e, 10-a

## 150.

1-l, 2-u, 3-m, 4-v, 5-a, 6-w, 7-n, 8-b, 9-o, 10-c, 11-f, 12-d, 13-q, 14-e, 15-r, 16-x, 17-p, 18-y, 19-g, 20-z, 21-h, 22-t, 23-i, 24-s, 25-j, 26-k

## 151.

1. No. 1
2. No. 24
3. No. 44
4. Babe Ruth, Lou Gehrig, Joe DiMaggio, Mickey Mantle, Bill Dickey and Yogi Berra, Whitey Ford, and Casey Stengel, respectively
5. No. 32: Jimmy Brown, Cleveland Browns; Elston Howard, New York Yankees; and Sandy Koufax, Los Angeles Dodgers
6. No. 76 was Marion Motley, No. 77 was Red Grange

## 152.

1. Kentucky
2. Abilene Christian
3. New Hampshire
4. Northwestern
5. Davidson
6. Northern Michigan
7. Weber State
8. Villanova
9. Arizona
10. Kansas State

## 153.

c

## 154.

1-F-d; 2-G-g; 3-A-e; 4-I-h; 5-B-j; 6-J-i; 7-C-c; 8-D-b; 9-H-f; 10-E-a